Print. Cut. Create!

art to print for all kinds of projects

JennaDisc No.1

Live the creative life! It's as close as your printer. Just put your JennaDisc in, press "print," and out will flow pages of art, patterns, and designs to create a world full of projects for every season.

Jenna's Studio *the seasons*, is a book and CD-Rom that will inspire you to clip, glue, paint, and create through the entire year. Your JennaDisc contains 72 pages of art and patterns you can use over and over again!

This book is packed full of projects. The photography is crisp and clean, the directions are simple to understand, and the projects are quick. The kids will love the holiday projects, you will love the versatility, the fun ideas and best of all — you won't have to drive to the store every time you need another paper. Just press "print" and everything you need is ready in a flash.

Jenna Lynne is an artist who continually surprises us with new design styles, more art for every season, and creative crafts. Leisure Arts is proud to share her unique talent with you. Welcome to Jenna's Studio.

Jenna's Studio *the seasons*
by Jenna Lynne

Crafting Assistant, Lori Sasaki
Photography Consultant, Victor Zuniga
Supplies Coordinator, Rhoda Nazanin

LEISURE ARTS, INC.
EDITORIAL STAFF
VICE PRESIDENT AND EDITOR-IN-CHIEF Sandra Graham Case
EXECUTIVE DIRECTOR OF PUBLICATIONS Cheryl Nodine Gunnells
SENIOR PUBLICATIONS DIRECTOR Susan White Sullivan
DIRECTOR OF DESIGNER RELATIONS Debra Nettles
SENIOR DESIGN DIRECTOR Cyndi Hansen
CRAFT PUBLICATIONS DIRECTOR Deb Moore
DIRECTOR OF RETAIL MARKETING Stephen Wilson
SPECIAL PROJECTS DIRECTOR Susan Frantz Wiles
SENIOR ART OPERATIONS DIRECTOR Jeff Curtis
ART PUBLICATIONS DIRECTOR Rhonda Shelby
ART IMAGING DIRECTOR Mark Hawkins
IMAGING TECHNICIANS Stephanie Johnson and Mark Potter
PUBLISHING SYSTEMS ADMINISTRATOR Becky Riddle
PUBLISHING SYSTEMS ASSISTANTS Clint Hanson, Josh Hyatt, and John Rose

BUSINESS STAFF
CHIEF OPERATING OFFICER Tom Siebenmorgen
VICE PRESIDENT, SALES AND MARKETING Pam Stebbins
DIRECTOR OF SALES AND SERVICES Margaret Reinold
VICE PRESIDENT, OPERATIONS Jim Dittrich
COMPTROLLER, OPERATIONS Rob Thieme
RETAIL CUSTOMER SERVICE MANAGER Stan Raynor
PRINT PRODUCTION MANAGER Fred F. Pruss

Produced for Leisure Arts by Jenna Lynne. www.jennalynne.com, ©2005 by Jenna Lynne.

Printed in the U.S.A.

International Standard Book Number 1-57486-538-2
10 9 8 7 6 5 4 3 2 1

72 Pages of Art to Live the Creative Life!

Dear Friends,

I am continually impressed with the variety of papers, fabrics, canvases, vellums, decals, and other media your inkjet printer can accept. Better yet, YOU can use all these wonderful papers to create masterpieces of all types. Let your imagination soar. This book comes with a JennaDisc of seasonal art I painted for you to use in a variety of ways. Try scrapbooking papers, greeting cards, gift tags, sachets, pillows, picture frames, decorative towels, fancy sandals, gift boxes, ornaments, and limitless other projects.

Your JennaDisc is the beginning to a year full of art, crafts, projects, and fun. I have filled the enclosed CD-Rom with as many pages of my art as possible — 72 to be exact. You can use this art for every seasonal project from Valentine's Day gift boxes to Halloween Kitchen Witches, Christmas Cards to Easter dishes. Your JennaDisc holds endless crafting and creating possibilities.

The JennaDisc works with both Mac and PC platforms. For complete instructions to use your JennaDisc (it's easy!) turn to page 6.

Take my art and make your own masterpieces! Experiment and have fun. I want to see what you use your JennaDisc for, so email me a photo of what you create. My email address is Create@jennalynne.com.

I hope our creative alliance becomes a habit. Please visit my website to see what other books, scrapbooking products and great craft ideas are awaiting you!

All the best,

Jenna

Jenna Lynne
www.jennalynne.com
email: Create@jennalynne.com

Special Thanks to so many

Joseph, who tolerates me and understands why I work into the wee hours of the morning. Nicholas, who fills life with joy. Mom, who taught me everything. Dad, who makes us all laugh. Grandma, the most God-filled expression of Love. Joni L., who inspires so many and is a trustworthy friend.

Cyndi H., who believes in me. This entire book would never have been, if it weren't for her. Sandra C., who listens with wisdom. Cheryl G., who cuts to the chase.

To Tami L.-F., who pushes me. Paul T., who wisely gave me my first design job. Marty S., who gave me a start. Victor Z., who knows his cameras. Dawn P., who inspires with her ice skating and coaching. Rhoda N., who is growing into an amazing woman. Jon N., for computers and patience. Lori S., who cuts very straight lines and always has a smile.
Thank you all.

Table of Contents

Jenna's Studio
the seasons

art to print for projects, entertaining & celebrations

How To use your JennaDisc 6

Autumn 46

Wintertime 60

How to use your JennaDisc
(it's easy, I promise!)

Welcome to the wonderful world of creating!

It's so exciting for me to be able to share my love for design with you through the special JennaDisc that's included with this book. On the JennaDisc you'll find loads of papers, art for clipping, and designs that can be used for the projects in the book and so much more! Let your creativity flow and let me know what fantastic ways you've found to use the art...you can email them to me at Create@jennalynne.com.

All the images on the JennaDisc are PDF files which stands for Portable Document Format. The files are easily opened using **Adobe Acrobat Reader.** If you don't have Acrobat Reader on your computer, you can install it from the CD or download it for free at http://www.adobe.com/. It's really easy to download and they have step-by-step instructions on how to do it.

MAC or PC, you've got it made with the JennaDisc. This disc works with all computers.

Using your JennaDisc is as easy as 1...2...3!

⬤ Step 1. Insert the JennaDisc into your computer's CD drive.

⬤ Step 2. Click on the file name that's indicated in the project instructions.

⬤ Step 3. Print the image on your inkjet printer and start creating!

Let the art of the seasons come to life

Special printing notes:
All the images are sized at 100% to fit the projects in the book. If you'd like to print them out at a larger or smaller size to fit your own creation, use the sizing function in your print dialog box to enlarge or reduce the image from its original size. Just remember, if you are enlarging, print preview your image before you print it out to make sure it still fits on the page.

Some of the files on the JennaDisc are larger than 8½" x 11" and have 11" x 17" in the file title. If your printer doesn't print 11" x 17", you should be able to go to your local copy center and have them print out the image. Please remember, most specialty papers like iron-on transfer paper are made specifically to use with an inkjet printer...make sure they use the right printer for your paper!

When developing this book with my publishers, we were very clear that the use of the JennaDisc had to be ultra-easy, for even those of us with little or no computer experience. For this very reason, we used the **Adobe Acrobat program, which most people already have installed on their computer, MAC or PC.**

Turn to Page 95 for a complete listing of all the files on your JennaDisc.

Other Jenna Lynne artful products and leaflets from Leisure Arts™ and Memories in the Making™.

From Jenna's Studio to you

Live the creative life! This book comes with a CD-Rom full of seasonal art painted by Jenna Lynne. You can print all the art you need to make a year's worth of projects. Use your JennaDisc to create masterpieces, one project at a time.

JennaDisc
No.1
art to print
for all kinds
of projects

Designs for Halloween

Art for Beach Babes

BBQ Graphics

Christmas Collections

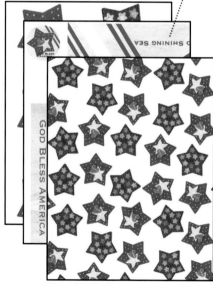

Patriotic Patterns

Asian Artistry

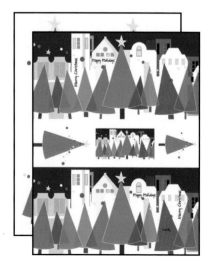

Holiday Papers

Vintage Valentine Art

Ooolala Girls

Fanciful Florals for Decor

Here is a sampling of the 72 images on the JennaDisc included with this book.

Snowman Patterns

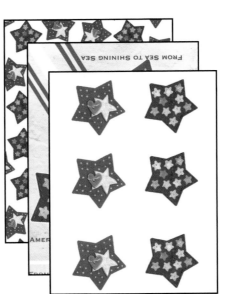

Americana Art

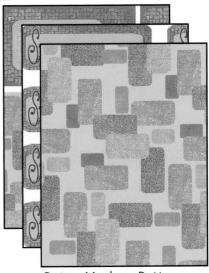

Autumn Artistry

Santa Claus Styles

9

Retro-Modern Patterns

I promise to show you infinite patience. I promise to always show you to ... you. I promise to laugh with ... snuggle every morning. I prom... butterfly kisses and bear h... encourage your spirit. I pion...

your tears. I promise to let you jump on the be... I promise to love you forever with my whole heart. I

Springtime

promise to show you the sites of the universe, the ... lebrate you in a... ...te patience.

I promise ... promise to alw... you. I prom... snuggle every...

... alw...

... prom...

... every.

... kisses and bear hugs. I promise to ... butterfly kis...

encourage yo...

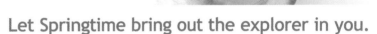

the art of the season

Let Springtime bring out the explorer in you.

Spring sunshine always inspires designs of exotic, bold colors and embellishments of grand proportion. Let the following pages inspire you to travel through a season full of intricate Easter eggs, delicate invitations, stylish Valentine totes, and vintage collectibles. Achieving world-class style has never been easier, so leave your passport at home and start creating with your JennaDisc.

→For complete instructions to use your JennaDisc, turn to page 6…It's easy!

A Vintage Valentine

Can you hear the birds chirp first thing in the morning? Have you looked for the daffodil's first green shoots? Spring is in the air and our favorite projects mix vintage charm with all the latest in ribbons, bows, and newfangled technologies to create old-fashioned collectibles. Old is in...and you're way ahead of your time!

—▷For complete instructions to use your **JennaDisc**, turn to page 6.

Materials

Heart-shaped paper mâché boxes

Blank newsprint

Craft glue

Soft paintbrush

Items to embellish your box: grosgrain ribbons, paper roses, embroidery floss and perle cotton

Step 1. From the JennaDisc, print **VINTAGEcollage** onto newsprint. Crumple the paper and flatten it out. Mix 2 parts craft glue with 1 part water.

Step 2. Paint the box and the lid with the glue mixture. Overlapping papers as desired and trimming the pieces to fit, cover the box and lid with the papers...the bumps and imperfections will add texture! Paint over the box and lid with a thin layer of the glue mixture and allow to dry.

Step 3. See the finishing details for each box, *below*, to add the embellishments.

Bouquet Heart Box

Antique paper roses from the wedding section of the craft store make this box quick and easy! Wrap the stems of three roses with floral tape. Tie a length of old lace and some embroidery floss over the tape, then glue the bouquet to the box.

Floret Box

A modern version of a classic lapel pin adds a vintage touch to this box. Start by punching holes every ¹⁄₂" around the lid, then stitch through the holes using perle cotton. Use a running stitch to gather one edge of a grosgrain ribbon length into a circle. Glue on a piece of beaded trim and top it off with an antique paper rose. Glue the floret to the box.

—▷ *See Resources, page 84, for product information.*

Grosgrain Accents

The latest trend is all about grosgrain ribbon! This classic pink version is made modern with small white stitches along the edges. Match it with old lace pieces and the result is a wonderful mix of Grandma's antiques mixed with today's most chic accent.

a few of my favorite things

I promise to show you infinite patience. I promise to snuggle you every morning and laugh with you every day. I promise to encourage your spirit. I promise to wipe away your tears. I promise to give you butterfly kisses and bear hugs. I promise to show you the gifts of the universe, to celebrate the gift you are to the world and to delight in your discovering God's diversity. I promise to let you jump on the bed.   — *Jenna,* in a letter to her son

These are the words written on the pillow (above). Make something special for a child or a mother-to-be with phrases to cherish. All the art you need is on your JennaDisc.

14

Grosgrain Bow Pillow

Materials:

4 sheets colorfast inkjet fabric, white

3/4 yard of 7/8"w grosgrain ribbon

1/2 yard of fabric for pillow back

poly foam filling

button and heavy-duty thread

⟶ Use a 1/2" seam allowance for all sewing.

● **Step 1:** Print two copies of **VINTAGEtext** and one copy each of **VINTAGEheart** and **VINTAGEroses** from your JennaDisc onto the inkjet fabric. Follow the package instructions to dry and iron the images. Centering the image, cut each piece to 8" x 8"; remove the paper.

● **Step 2:** Press the seams to one side before sewing then sew the pieces together as shown. Pillow back: Cut a square of fabric the same size as the pillow top. Press one edge of each piece 1/2" to the wrong side. Matching right sides and pressed edges and

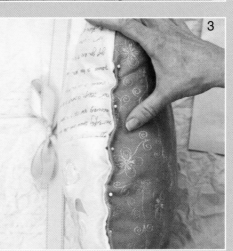

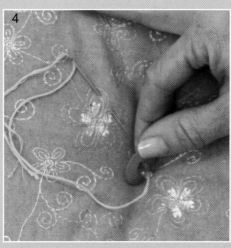

leaving the pressed edges open for inserting the filling, sew along the raw edges of the pillow.

● **Step 3:** Turn the pillow right side out and press. Fill the pillow with poly foam filling and sew the opening closed.

● **Step 4:** Using heavy-duty thread and sewing through the button on the back side of the pillow, stitch through the pillow to cinch the center; knot the threads on the front to secure. Tie the ribbon into a bow and tack it to the pillow.

⟶ *See Resources, page 84, for product information.*

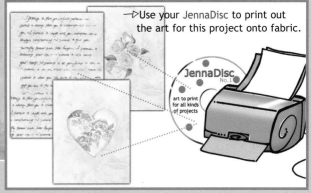

⟶Use your JennaDisc to print out the art for this project onto fabric.

JennaDisc No.1

art to print for all kinds of projects

Be Mine Backpacks

What do you give to someone who has you by the heartstrings?
A Valentine backpack, of course! Packed with special sentiments, these
knapsacks are made from vibrant oilcloths and ribbons. Print out the patterns
from your JennaDisc then create to your heart's desire!

For complete instructions to use your JennaDisc, turn to page 6.

Heart Pattern 1

place black line on
fold of fabric
and cut on the blue line

Strawberry Leaves Pattern
cut 2

Heart Pattern 2

Strawberry Pattern
cut 2

JennaDisc
No.1

art to print
for all kinds
of projects

Strawberry Backpack

Materials:

2/3 yard green check oilcloth, 1/2 yard red oilcloth, scrap of white oilcloth or fabric, scrap of lime green felt, 11" each of aqua and green pom-pom trim, 11" of white braided trim, 6" green cord, fiberfill, fabric glue, pinking shears, monofilament sewing thread

Step 1. Print the following patterns from your JennaDisc: **Heart_Pattern1, Heart_Pattern2, Strawberry_Leaves** and **Strawberry_Pattern.** Tape patterns together as shown on patterns. Using pinking shears, cut 2 heart shapes from green check oilcloth. Cut 1 heart shape from red oilcloth 1/2" larger on all sides than pattern.

Step 2. Center and glue one green heart to the red heart. Stack and glue the pom-pom trim and braided trim to the green heart shape, as shown. This is the front piece of the backpack.

Step 3. Cut two 24" x 4" strips of green check oilcloth for the straps. Fold the long edges of each into thirds, slightly overlapping at the center. Sew edges in place.

Step 4. Referring to the pattern for placement, pin one end of each strap to the wrong side of the front piece. Adjust the length to fit your child and pin the loose ends of the straps as indicated on the pattern.

Step 5. Matching wrong sides and sandwiching strap ends between the front and back pieces, pin, then stitch around the edges, leaving an opening between the straps at the top of the backpack.

Step 6. Using pinking shears, cut 2 strawberry shapes from red oilcloth. With wrong sides together, stitch around the outer edge, leaving a small opening. Lightly stuff with fiberfill and sew the opening closed. Using the seed pattern, cut 3 seeds from white oilcloth or fabric and glue to the strawberry shape, as shown. Cut 2 strawberry leaf patterns from lime green felt. Stitch around the outer edge, leaving a small opening. Lightly stuff with fiberfill and sew the opening closed. Tack a loop of the green cord to the leaves. Glue the leaves to the strawberry and the strawberry to the backpack.

→ See Resources, page 84, for product information.

Be Mine Ladybug Backpack

Materials:

2/3 yard berry print oilcloth, 1/4 yard red oilcloth, scrap of lime green felt, 1"w kelly green grosgrain ribbon, 5/8"w lime green grosgrain ribbon, 6" green cord, 8" white pom-pom trim, fiberfill, 2 moving eyes, 2 small and 2 medium fun foam hearts, fabric glue, pinking shears, monofilament sewing thread, and clear vinyl

Step 1. Print the following patterns from your JennaDisc: **Heart_Pattern1, Heart_Pattern2,** and **Strawberry_Leaves.** Tape patterns together as shown on patterns. Using pinking shears, cut 2 heart shapes from the berry print oilcloth.

Step 2. Stack and glue the ribbons and pom-pom trim to one of the heart shapes, as shown. This is the front piece of the backpack.

Step 3. Cut two 24" x 4" strips of berry print oilcloth for the straps. Fold the long edges of each into thirds, slightly overlapping at the center. Sew edges in place.

Step 4. Referring to the pattern for placement, pin one end of each strap to the wrong side of the front piece.

Adjust the length to fit your child and pin the loose ends of the straps as indicated on the pattern.

Step 5. Matching wrong sides and sandwiching strap ends between the front and back pieces, pin, then stitch around the edges, leaving an opening between the straps at the top of the backpack.

Step 6. Using pinking shears, cut two 5" dia. ladybug body shapes from red oilcloth. With wrong sides together, stitch around the outer edge, leaving a small opening. Lightly stuff with fiberfill and sew the opening closed. Stitch lines for the head and wings, as shown in photo (*right*). Attach moving eyes and draw bug details with a permanent marker.

Step 7. Center and glue the small foam fun hearts to the medium hearts. Cut 2 small strawberry leaf patterns from green felt and glue to the hearts, as shown in photo (*below*). Add seeds with a permanent marker. Knot the ends of the green cord and spot-glue the knots to the tops of the strawberries. Sandwich the strawberries between 2 pieces of clear vinyl and stitch closed in a heart shape. Do not sew over the green cord. With pinking shears, trim away excess vinyl. Tack

the center of the cord to the backpack, as shown.

heart's delight

Heart Rendering

Create heart-stopping edible art for all your sweethearts. Draw onto melt-in-your-mouth cookie forms with edible ink pens, place onto frosted cookies, and they're ready! Now you know what they mean by "Heart's Desire."

Kids love this Valentine's Day yummy art project. Served up with strawberries and laughs, it's a heart-felt afternoon project for all ages.

Heart in your Hand

Create incredible, edible cookies! Try using an architect's circle template from the office supply store, and make your own circle patterns. Write words of seasonal sentiment on your cookies. Below are some fun designs I did the other day with the kids. What will you design?

Edible ink pens make delightful cookies!

Heartland

Discover (and devour) edible cookie forms (*right*). Made of cornstarch and water, then formed into thin sheets or shapes ready for coloring, these are your canvases for incredible, edible cookies. The pens are filled with edible inks, too.

1 Put a layer of frosting on heart-shaped cookies. **2** Using edible ink pens, have the kids draw on the heart-shaped forms. **3** Simply pull the finished art off the backing, lay onto the cookie and it's ready to... well... disappear.

Kopykake, a small company in Southern California, makes all the products used here. See page 87.

19

Extravagant

Lavishly decorated Ukrainian eggs, dating back thousands of years before Christ, were an integral part of their festival of Spring. The most intricately decorated eggs were made by drawing on the shells with hot beeswax using a tiny funnel attached to a wooden handle, a traditional tool called a kystka. Come explore this fascinating method of egg design using modern tools, techniques, and waxes.

Eggs to Exhibit

Exceptionally beautiful and truly one of my favorite spring artistic endeavors!

Materials: an abundance of dry, dyed eggs that have been brought to room temperature, batik hot wax pen (see Resources, page 84), silver and gold and other colors of crayons to coordinate with the colors of your eggs.

● Before you begin working on your eggs, practice with the batik pen on scrap paper...these tools can be tricky! You have to pay close attention to the temperature of the wax. Too cool, it won't flow...too hot, it pours out quickly. You may need to plug and unplug your pen to adjust the temperature as you work.

● Step 1. Melt small pieces of crayon in the batik pen. You can use solid colors or mix a color with the silver or gold to add shimmer.

● Step 2. Working in small sections, use the pen to draw on the eggs. Designs based on floral patterns, swirls, and dots work best. Experiment and have fun! Allow the wax to harden before you move to the next section. A spoon works well to cradle the egg while the wax hardens.

● If you make a smudge or don't like a small section of your design, don't fret. Let the wax dry, then use a sharp craft knife to scrape off the wax...you're ready to start anew.

▭▷ I recommend this craft for adults only. The hot pen and wax have to be handled with extreme caution.

21

Spring Pleaser

Forget casual dining — opt for scones and raspberry tea or freshly squeezed orange juice and crumb cake. Anything served on this stunning tableware proves you can still serve with style and class. The setting may have been created for Easter, but it's perfect for any elegant gathering. Live lavishly and let the artistic expression of the season bloom.

Citrina Design Tableware

Inspired by exotic patterns from other cultures and modern colors of our locale, this set of dishes is the perfect nesting place for your exceptional eggs. The process is simple, and the results are out of this world. For complete instructions, *turn to page 86*.

Print the **Citrina** files from your JennaDisc to make this project.

eggspress yourself

We use our hands for both creation and expression. The hand might hold a pencil as it swoops across the page, or wave in greeting to a passing neighbor. You might use just the fingers of one hand to count your blessings or you might use hands, arms, and shoulders to embrace the ones you love. When you create handmade cards, you use your hands to communicate your feelings through your creations. So go ahead — eggspress yourself.

Eggsplosion

Print the various **Cintrina** papers. Glue 3" squares of each pattern to white cardstock. Cut out egg shapes, set aside. Fold a 10" x 6" piece of light blue cardstock in half. Stitch on an arc with lavender thread. Using a large needle, thread with pastel embroidery thread (pink, yellow, white) and sew 3 separate bows into the arch. Glue the eggs to the blue cardstock at the base of the bows. Add your greeting, in this case the word, "eggstra," and on the inside of the card write, "Happy Easter to you."

→ *See Resources, page 84, for product information.*

Eggxotic

Artist Trading Cards: Read about them on the next page, and create your own. Trade, share, collect. To make them, print the various **Citrina** papers from your JennaDisc onto matte heavyweight paper. To make the carrot, cut out the shape of the carrot, set aside. Cut 2 pieces of lime green craft wire and curl as shown. Glue them to a piece of cardstock the size and shape of a playing card. Mount the carrot over the wires with an adhesive dot. Write the word "Spring" and draw dots $1/4$" apart across the top and bottom.

Lower card: Read instructions above. Augment by cutting sun rays out of various **Citrina** papers. Mount the center circle with adhesive dot and add text.

Eggsuberant

Follow the directions on page 89 for detailed instructions. Isn't it wonderful?

Eggcite me

Start with the wings of yellow cardstock to make this chick. Add a circle of **Citrina2** paper, then a bowtie of yellow cardstock. Use an adhesive dot to attach a round head. Draw eyes and beak. Mold boots out of clay, dry and use embroidery thread for legs. Mount on cardstock, then onto **Citrina1** paper, then on blue cardstock. Add text "Peep" underneath boots.

cards as gifts, to trade, to collect

The greeting card: a way of welcoming, a gesture of kindness, an expression of sentiment that dates back to the the first papers pounded out of papyrus thousands of years ago near the Nile River. **Artist Trading Cards** (ATC's) are a modern expression mixing handmade art and expression. The size of a playing card, individually made and traded amongst the likeminded, ATC's are gaining popularity, bringing together those who cherish the gifts of both greeting and creating.

Eggstra Special

Create a hoppin' nice card using Citrina papers! Print out the file **Citrina1** onto textured paper. Make a square card out of the paper. Freehand draw a bunny head onto pink paper and cut out. Using 26-gauge gold wire, cut 6 whiskers and glue them to the bunny. Using adhesive dots, adhere the bunny to the card.

Eggspert

Citrina papers make this Springtime Artist Trading Card (ATC) a piece of carrot cake. See similar cards on the opposite page for details.

Creative Eggsplosion

Use your sewing machine and make squiggle stitches all around. Print **Citrina3** from your JennaDisc, cut out an oval, mount onto blue cardstock, and trim a $1/8$" border. Glue a bow from embroidery thread to the top of the egg. Mount the egg using a self-adhesive 3-D dot to stitched piece.

Eggsquisite

Make a 4" x 6" card from **Citrina2** paper. Adhere a smaller piece of pink cardstock to card. Cut a circle of light yellow cardstock for chick's head. Cut a small triangle for beak; draw eyes on. Cut a body for the chick out of bright yellow paper. Glue chick to card. Make an egg shell out of **Citrina2** paper. Glue egg shell shape to green cardstock and trim a $1/8$" border. Use self-adhesive 3-D dot to mount eggshell to chick. For grass, cut a 3" x $1/2$" piece of green cardstock. Make fringe cuts across the top, curl and glue to card. Add text and pink dots freehand.

25

It's a Pampering Party!

(also known as "Girls' Night In")

The girls in my family (4 of us) say an evening in for *"Ooolala Pampering"* is like a weekend spent with our well-traveled froo-froo Grandmother Irene who taught us from an early age that orange sticks are for manicures and that the sunshine will ruin your skin. She taught us the marvels of pedicures, gave us her old high-heeled shoes to play dress-up, and took us to fancy restaurants for lunch. All girls need a mentor to introduce them to the Girl's Club of Curlers, Tweezers & Facials. Now it's your turn! Discover the splendor of a spa night at home with your best friends, sharing stories, fingernail polish and savoring the good life. Indeed, Grandma Irene would be so proud.

Make an Invitation

Glamour rules with this corset invitation! Unlace it to reveal a fancy, folded invitation with pull-up inserts. (*See photo opposite page.*) For complete directions, turn to page 88.

Beaded Beauty

What a fun project! Make glitzy bracelets while giggling. Full directions on page 89.

Easy Place Cards

Embellish these 3-dimensional frame sets with sparkles, flowers, and glitterati! They're called *"Suspenders,"* and you can get them at your scrapbooking store. Use them as place cards, and place photos of your guest in the frame. See Resources, page 84.

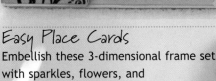

Party Perfect

As soon as your friends pop open the invitation, they'll know it's special. Create these small party favors and nibbles beforehand and prepare some activities for the gathering for a perfect night in, indeed!

Glamorous Tabletop

Buy napkin rings and turn them into glitzy bits of art. Make tufted place mats out of dupioni silk and fancy beads. Directions on page 88.

Double Dipping!

Follow the directions on the box of *Dolci Frutta* and make chocolate dipped strawberry delights. Stunning! See Resources, page 84.

27

Balm Shell

If your guest bathroom is any reflection of who you really are, then I say let your glamorous side show through. Your guests will love it, too. A powder room replete with pink, lime and tangerine is sure to please. Now is the time to turn your bathroom into a colorful celebration. Be a bathing beauty!

Balm Shell Towel Set

Materials:

1 sheet colorfast inkjet fabric, white

grosgrain ribbons, rickrack, satin ribbon, pom-pom trim

1 white bath towel, 1 white hand towel

1/2" roll of iron-on adhesive

Step 1: Bath Towel *(right)*: Print 1 copy of file **Balmshell** from your JennaDisc onto colorfast inkjet transfer fabric. Peel the paper off the back. Follow package directions for colorfast treatment. Cut the image out, leaving 1/4" of white border around the edges. Center as shown, 4" from the bottom edge of the towel. Sew to the towel. Trim off white edge.

Step 2: Using iron-on adhesive, fuse various ribbons together as shown. Use rickrack, satin, grosgrain. Be creative.

Step 3: Sew various ribbons and pom-poms to the towel.

Small Hand Towel: For the bow accent *(above)*, tie a grosgrain ribbon bow and tack it at the knot for stability. Then, loop satin ribbons through the loops of the bow and glue the satin ribbons together with a dot of fabric glue. When dry, use iron-on adhesive to adhere to a wide grosgrain ribbon. Embellish with pom-pom trim and rickrack ribbon.

⟶▷ Note: These towels are for decoration rather than for the rigors of washing machines. Make them for show, and use your other towels to dry your hair! See Resources, page 84.

Print the file **Balmshell** from your JennaDisc to make this project.

Bathroom Beauties
for all Ooolala Girls

Your bathroom is more than just a place to leave behind wet towels and put on some lipstick. It's your personal haven. And the "Ooolala Girls" I love drawing are such a fun way to make your beauty sanctuary sensational. I have used loads of bright colors to surround each sensational girl.

3 Framed Girls: Print out the three OooLaLa Girls images from your JennaDisc. The files are named **Navigate**, **Radiate** and **Meditate**. Print them onto inkjet canvas. Cut them to fit 5" x 7" canvases with ¹/₂" overlap. Score the canvas images to fit the frame then glue onto the canvas with fabric glue *(below)*. Finish them off by gluing a ribbon around the edges, if you'd like.

Walkin' on Sunshine
in the hottest little sandals

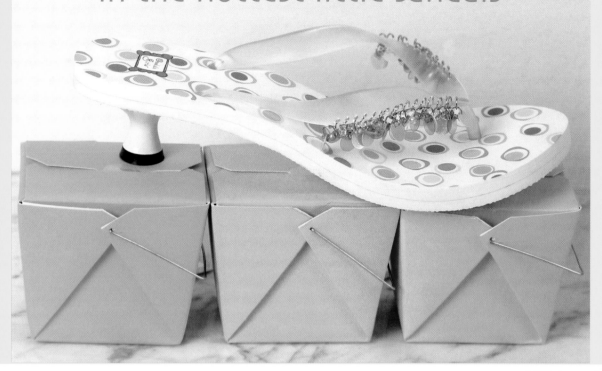

Have a Pedicure Party!

Invite over your friends and tell them to bring a new pair of bright flip-flops (and 2 pair of chain-nose pliers, if they have them). Have jump rings and beads ready. Surprise them with this clever project to do while waiting for their toenail polish to dry. Serve fresh juices and munch on popcorn. Expect a good time for all!

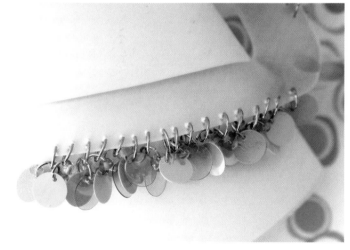

Walking on Sunshine Sandals

Materials: 100 7mm jump rings, 2 pair chain nose pliers, beads with large openings and flat disc beads

Directions: Using a tiny scrapbooking hole punch, make a row of holes down the edge of the band of the flip-flop, approximately 1/8" apart *(above)*. Insert jump rings in each of the holes, but don't close them. Set aside. Open more jump rings and slide on 3 beads and 2 disc beads, alternating. Close jump rings. See photo *(left)*. Slide the closed beaded jump rings onto the open sandal jump rings, close them with pliers. Paint your toenails and show off!

→ *See Resources, page 84, for product information.*

31

love • cherish • mother

Zen & Now

Asian design is based on clarity and refinement. The purpose is to create something divine from the most simple of elements...just like your mother did with you. Once a tiny baby in her arms with a few simple needs, she guided and shaped you into who you are today. Combining this simple art form with the delicate Asian papers and elements from your JennaDisc, you can create this serene Mother's Day gift set to tell her how much she means to you...Zen & Now.

Asian Artistry

JennaDisc No.1

art to print for all kinds of projects

The day I chose this theme must have been particularly serene. At the art store, I gravitated to the Asian papers section, mixed and matched rice papers and scrapbooking papers, then added my own art to create this Mother's Day collection. Using readily available wooden trays and boxes, Asian embellishments and the **Kimono Art** and **Asian Papers** on your JennaDisc, you'll have a tranquil time making these exquisite Mother's Day gifts.

Print the following files; **Asian1**, **Asian2**, **Asian3**, **Asian4**, **Kimono1**, and **Kimono2**.

The card *(above left)* is accented with an embossed metal tag...roughen up the surface of the tag with a file before you emboss it. Texturize the paper with acrylic and metallic copper paints. Accent with additional papers from the art supply or stationery store.

The framed art *(above)* is created by layering papers printed from your JennaDisc. Silk ribbons, Asian coins, mesh pieces, and embossed metal tags add the details to this dark cherry stained tray. It's simply elegant!

Give a gift with inner beauty and artful touches from your JennaDisc. The box *(right)* looks stunning and was easier than you can imagine. Line the walls of your box with pieces of cardstock covered with Asian papers from your JennaDisc. Next, line the lid and bottom of the box with pieces of posterboard wrapped with silk. Add a layered paper accent and an embossed metal tag in the lid. To keep the lid from opening too far, simply glue ribbon from the lid to the box. Give a gift with inner beauty and artful touches using your JennaDisc.

⌐▷ *See Resources, page 84, for product information.*

FROM SEA TO SHINING SEA

Summertime

GOD BLESS AMERICA

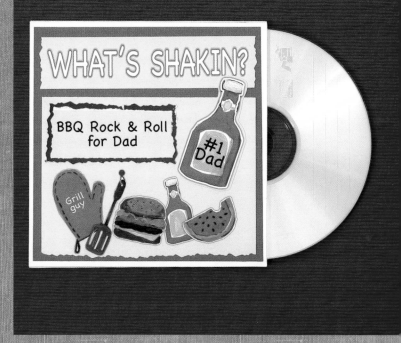

Although Summertime is limited

to a certain number of days, it is a timeless season of days at the beach, BBQ sauce, and sun hats. It's a time to enjoy the warm weather with a cool drink. These pages are full of time-off projects, memory keepers, and well-seasoned recipes. Call the neighbors over for a Pool Party, plan for Father's Day and celebrate the 4th of July. Your JennaDisc contains limitless summertime art to use for all these gatherings. When the season slowly draws to a close, make a seasonal Memory Book to enjoy time and again, with patterns and art from Jenna Lynne.

the art of the season

A Patriotic Party

I think the National Pastime for women should be Making Things. Think of the things that **women** enjoy making, like flower arrangements, making people happy, making merry, making cakes or curtains, making elegant dinners, and, on occasion, **making it through the day**. It's in our nature to create. (Mother Nature had a say in that, I'm sure.) So, take some time out for creating — make it simple, complex, red, white or blue. It's my hope my art will inspire you to **make something as truly special as you are.**

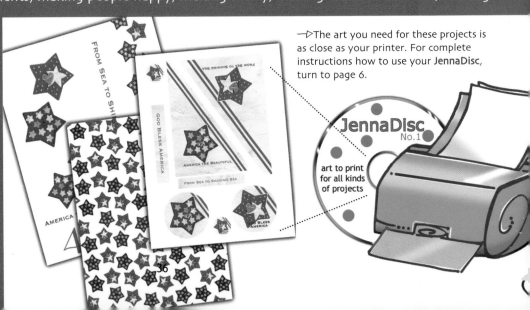

—▷The art you need for these projects is as close as your printer. For complete instructions how to use your **JennaDisc**, turn to page 6.

JennaDisc No.1

art to print for all kinds of projects

THE STATE OF THE REUNION

SUMMER can best be described with two words: **Get Together!** Make it a time to reunite yourself with warm weather parties and cool refreshments! Call everyone together for a patriotic party with a nautical flair. Make red, white and blue boating place cards, a watermelon flower arrangement, starry coasters, and more. The State of the Reunion will never look better!

Nautical Place Card Boats

Using your JennaDisc to print out these patriotic images onto fabric, you can turn a simple wooden boat from the hobby store into a place card fit for the high seas! For complete instructions, turn to page 90.

High Seas Coasters

Top a simple shell coaster with a classic American symbol, the star. Print this design out from your JennaDisc onto decal paper, apply, and when dry, spray with clear acrylic gloss. The decal becomes translucent and the unique shell pattern comes through. See page 86.

Rise to the Occasion

Take a cake riser and twist on capiz shell stars for a patriotic flavor. See Resources, page 84.

Seeing Stars!

Do something out of the ordinary! Cut watermelon into stars with cookie cutters and turn them into a fireworks centerpiece worthy of oooh's and ahhh's!
See page 91 for specifics.

Old Glory Days

The only way to have a friend
is to be one.
—Ralph Waldo Emerson

FROM SEA TO SHINING SEA

OREGON TRIP
2005

Memory Books

Your JennaDisc contains many of the patterns, designs, and icons used in these Memory Books. Stars and stripes, time-worn colors, and background papers are ready to use by simply sliding the JennaDisc into your computer. Print the files **4thBigStars**, **4thSails**, **4thScatter** and **4thSmallStars**. Try woven or handmade papers, canvas or fabric for a multitude of textures and styles. For a listing of Products and Resources, turn to page 84.

I cannot even imagine
where I would be today
were it not for that handful
of friends who have given
me a heart full of joy.
—Charles R. Swindoll

With a non-stop giggle and a quirky sense of humor, you can bet our Karen is the life of the party. Always!

Karen

4th of July
with the family

I used to think my mother was corny when she'd say things like, "If I could only save this moment forever," or "I'm too old to get in the swimming pool." Now, I get it. If I could amass hugs from my child, always feel the softness of his hand as it slips into mine, constantly smell the sweet scent of his face when he has just woken up. If it were possible, I would stockpile all those sensations. As life has it, however, we can not backlog moments. We can only store some momentos, photos, and relive those cherished specks of time via our memory. It's no wonder why Memory Books are so precious — for us to relive those hugs, sweet scents, and irreplaceable moments shared with the ones we love. Please, start a Memory Book soon...that is, AFTER you go jump in the swimming pool.

Faith in the Flag

Some years back, I took my 3 year-old son on a trip to visit Maura and Curtis, some friends in Indiana. We fed corn to the deer, made silly face masks, and baked lemon cakes. On the hour-long journey to the airport in Indianapolis to return home, we passed an old cemetery, overgrown with wheat and weeds. An abandoned flag hung from a tipping pole. It was ripped and barely holding on to the tether, reigning over a few graves. The fence was rusty and broken. My son got very upset to see a flag in such condition — because he was 3 years old — it was not easy to console him. Curtis, a retired minister, promised my son he'd replace the flag next time he came to that spot on the freeway. I never thought for a minute that Curtis was making that promise for any reason other than to quiet my anxious son. The long flight home and the return to real life blurred the memory of the neglected flag.

A month later, this photograph arrived in the mail. It is of Curtis raising Old Glory in replacement of the tattered flag that once hung over a small cemetery along the route from southern Indiana to Indianapolis. God Bless America. And God Bless Americans.

→Your JennaDisc holds all the art you need to make these All American Memory Book pages.
The file names are:
4thBigStars, 4thSails, 4thScatter & 4thSmallStars.

GOD BLESS AMERICA

WAVES, BABES & RAYS
Make a splash of a pool party for the babes! Let your **JennaDisc** help you create ALL the things pictured. Dive in — it's very easy and the kids will love to see their names all around!

Beach Babes!

Just add sunscreen!

Buy plastic soap dispensers, personalize them for the kids, and fill them with sunscreen. Print out tropical patterns from your JennaDisc and decorate sun hats, onesies, and bibs. Art to make serving trays, ice buckets, cups, sunscreen dispensers, and whatever else you want to decorate, is ready right now. Make some big waves and create!

→Jump right in! Personalize, decorate, and design yourself into a tide pool of delightful fun & sun items. *Directions, page 91. Resources, page 85.*

Memories to Hang on to!

Scrapbook the page and frame it — then transform it into a towel rack the kids will love

Scrapbooking for the walls!

Every image you need to create this delightful Memory Frame/Towel Rack is on your JennaDisc. If you choose to go the digital route, detailed instructions are opposite. If you wish to use original scrapbookers tools like craft knives and glue sticks, just print the following files and get started: **Beach_Big_Pink**, **Beach_Big_Blue**, **Beach_Suntan**, **Beach_Blue**, and **Beach_Pink**. Print, cut, and create! See page 93 for details.

Beach Babes Memory Frame
Go Photoshopping!

For the directions in this section, I assume you have a computer with Photoshop™ and have an intermediate understanding of the program. Digital Scrapbooking is growing more sophisticated and Photoshop™ is an amazing tool! I made this Memory Frame using Photoshop™ 7.0, and a printer that takes paper as large as 11"x 17". If you don't have an over-sized printer, save your file on a disc and go to your local copy store. See Resources, page 85, for specifics.

Open the file **Beach_Suntan** and either **Beach_Big_Blue** or **Beach_Big_Pink** (for boys or girls) from your JennaDisc into Photoshop™.

Create a new Photoshop™ file, size 10.75" x 10.75", 275 dpi. Name it MemoryFrame1, and save it. Drag the **Beach_Big_Blue** or **Beach_Big_Pink** image, using the move tool, into your new file. It should fit perfectly. If it does not fit perfectly, your file size is most likely incorrect. Go to Image-Image Size to recheck, and if incorrect, fix. You now have your background.

Since the final trimmed size of the paper will be 10" x 10", pull guides in $^6/_{16}$" all the way around, so the art you're creating doesn't fall outside those boundaries. After printed, you will trim off the extra area, called "bleed." Open the 3 photos you wish to use. Import them as new layers into your file. Make new guides at $1^1/_2$" horizontally and vertically to use as the guide for the photos. Make another guide at $7^1/_2$" from the top as the base of the big photo. Drag the main photo into the file. If it is too large, use your Rectangular Marquee Tool, hold down the shift key and make a square around the area you want to use of the photo. Go to Select-Inverse then Edit-Cut. That will leave you with the part of the photo you want to use. Edit-Free Transform your image, holding down the shift key, until it snaps into the new guide size. Name the layer Photo 1.

Add a DROP SHADOW: On the layer Photo 1, take your magic wand and click on the area OUTSIDE the photo. Go to Select-Inverse. In your Layers palette (bottom right) click on the arrow and choose New Layer. Name it Drop Shadow 1. Your active layer will now be the new layer, just what you want. Look at your palette and make sure the top color selected is white. Go to Select-Feather, when prompted, select 8 pixels for your feather radius. Go to Edit-Fill. Go to your Layers and pull Drop Shadow down one layer below the layer named Photo 1. You now have a white drop shadow. Link Photo 1 to Drop Shadow.

2 smaller images on right side: Pull guides to $7^1/_2$" and $9^3/_4$" from the left. Pull 3 new guides from the top to $3^3/_4$", 4" and $6^1/_4$". These are the guides for the 2 small photos. Open the photo files and drag them into the file. Name them Photo 2 and 3 as you make them separate layers. One at a time, Edit-Free Transform your images,

holding down the shift key, until they snap into the area of the guides. Add a drop shadow to both images, separately, naming the layers, Drop Shadow 2 and 3. Link the drop shadow layers to their photos.

Add the white band for beach icons: Open the file **Beach_Suntan** from your JennaDisc. Using your Rectangular Marquee tool, make a rectangle around the icons and drag them into your file. Add new guides at $7^3/_4$" and $9^1/_2$" from the top ruler. Edit-Transform the icon band to fit between the horizontal guides. Edit-Cut the extra white on the right and left edges of the white band. Go to Layers and select Duplicate Layer. Do that twice. Line up the top edge of the 3 layers along the guide, link them together (at Layers) and merge them (Merge-Linked). Your band is complete, and it should start and stop wider than your guides at 1" and 10". To add a green stripe around the icon band, take your magic wand outside the band area and click it, Select-Inverse. Choose a bright green color (75% cyan, 100% yellow), go to Edit-Stroke, width 9 pixels on center.

Add journaling, *as shown*, font Lemonade Bold, 12 point, in black. Move text to fit lower area of white icon band, inside guides. Add words, Happy, Curious, etc., using Barmeno 20 point, in green, in various places.

"Beach Boy!" text and Frame: From the file **Beach_Suntan**, using your lasso, select the Frame and drag it to your file. Using your magic wand, click on the white outer area and go to Edit-Cut. Add a Drop Shadow, making sure the color selected is black. Link and merge. Place as shown. Add the text "Beach Boy!" using the font Barmeno, 25 point, in a royal blue. Place in the center of the frame.

Name: Your font size will depend on the number of letters in the name. Here, 120 points of Barmeno was used. To outline font, here's a fun trick. Write the name in the font you choose, make it a hair smaller than you want it to be when finished. In Layers, add a new layer, name it Name Outline. Link it to the text layer. Merge the layers (Layer-Merge Linked). Your text layer is now an art layer and you can add your yellow outline the same way you added the green frame line on the white icon band (*above*).

Save your file in open layers. Before printing onto photo paper, flatten your image (Layer-Flatten) and save it as MemoryFrameFlat.tiff. Print the flattened image on photo paper. Trim to 10"x10" and mount on yellow cardstock. Place in white scrapbooking frame.

Paint wooden towel knobs as shown with white and lime green paint. Hot glue to the frame.

Have a splashing good summer!

Carded!

Invite folks over for a BBQ on Father's Day. Create a cool invitation (*above, right*) using papers printed from your JennaDisc. *See page 91 for details.*

Father's Day BBQ

1:00 on Sunday

Ribs and Rockin'

• hot dogs • soda pop • watermelon •

WHAT'S COOKIN?

What's Cookin', Dad?

Make a feast of Father's Day gifts — An apron, cards, a CD case for hot tunes, a placemat, and the best BBQ sauce this side of Texas!

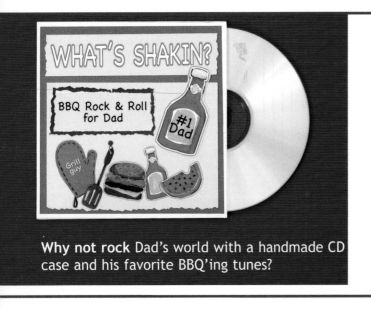

Why not rock Dad's world with a handmade CD case and his favorite BBQ'ing tunes?

Hittin' the BBQ Sauce Again! There are a few things in this life better than fathers, and this is one of them: my dad's Dynamite BBQ Sauce is rockin'! *Recipe, opposite page.*

WHAT'S COOKIN?

→ Turn to page 91 for complete instructions to make an apron (*above*), invite (*left*), and CD case (*below*).

Big Papa's Dynamite BBQ Sauce

My Grandfather DeAngeles, born in Italy, passed this chicken sauce recipe down to me via my father, Jack, who has perfected it into a dynamite BBQ sauce. Before sharing it here, I felt an obligation to get permission from my father. And! (Drum roll...) It is with great pleasure and generosity I offer you the most delicious, amazing, out of this world BBQ sauce ever. Thank you, Big Papa!

In a saucepan, simmer the following ingredients, stirring regularly: 1 can frozen Orange Juice Concentrate, $1/2$ stick butter, 1 cup brown sugar. Add $1/4$ cup of the following: soy sauce, ketchup, mustard, and whatever BBQ sauce you have. Add spices: garlic, rosemary, oregano & pepper, with dashes of worcestershire sauce and smoke flavoring. Simmer for 10 minutes and BBQ!

Saucy Art

All the BBQ art you need to make these Father's Day projects is on your JennaDisc. Print the files **BBQ_1-4** onto paper, inkjet canvas, fabric, and more. Cook up cards, place mats, an apron, a CD case cover, and more for a really hot celebration. No one deserves a party like Dad does, so throw him a big one!

→ *See Resources, page 84.*

Cookin' Up some Art!

→ Turn to page 6 for complete **JennaDisc** instructions.

45

Autumn

the art of the season

Fall into a season of changing colors,

windy weather, and the forgotten urge to bake bread, serve stew and make a cozy fire. Autumn welcomes so many holidays: Halloween and Thanksgiving as well as yearly Harvest Festivals, and school starting again. Let the art on your JennaDisc offer a windfall of

inspirations to handcraft a hearty home, make gifts for teachers, labels for your canned goods, kitchen witches and much more. The following pages hold a cornucopia of projects and bewitching ideas, so blow away your cares and create!

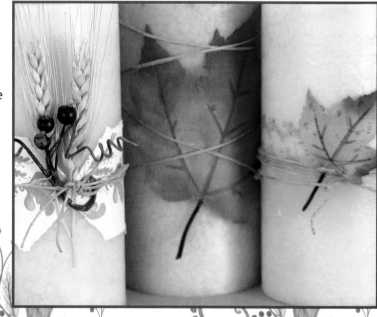

47

Falling on Card Times

Be Catty

Create a cool cat of a card with Jenna's art, buttons and thread! This feline face is set off by contrasting papers and seasonal colors. Make one for all your purrfect friends. See page 92.

Drive Me Batty

The perfect card for ALL husbands! "You drive me batty," says it all! This colorful card is sure to please everyone who drives you a little nuts. See page 92 for instructions.

Print. Cut. Create.

From your JennaDisc, print the following files: Halloween_2 and Halloween_3 onto heavyweight matte or glossy photo paper.

Cut out various shapes.

Create. Turn to page 92 for detailed photos and instructions.

Materials:
Various papers in orange, copper and yellow
Orange and yellow fiber paper
Inkjet papers
White cardstock or lightweight poster board
Spray mount
Scrapbooking eyelets
Small buttons
Polka-dot ribbon
Small wooden signs
Small wooden frames
Crafting fibers and perle cotton
Scrapbooking glue
A rounded corner paper punch
Black pen
copper metallic paint, yellow paint

→See Resources, page 84.

Magic Spell It Out!
Little wooden tags sell "happy spells" for a mere nickel each. Make this cute card with Halloween papers, ribbons, buttons and a little magic. See page 92.

Pumpkin Face
Tie a polka-dotted ribbon to this happy pumpkin tag! Using deckle-edged scissors and plenty of bright yellow cardstock, you can craft this cheery card accented with Halloween papers from your JennaDisc. See page 92.

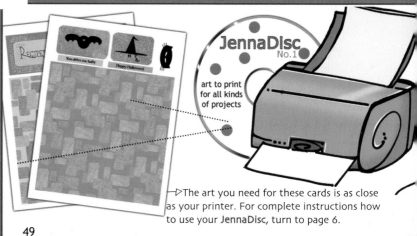

JennaDisc No.1
art to print for all kinds of projects

▷The art you need for these cards is as close as your printer. For complete instructions how to use your JennaDisc, turn to page 6.

What a Witch!

Top your pumpkin patch with the three cutest Kitchen Witches in town

KITCHEN WITCHES

are legendary "good luck" guardians of the kitchen. Descending from Norwegian or German folklore, the Kitchen Witch protects all who enter the home. It is also said they help protect the cook. Cakes, breads, and pastries will rise according to recipes. Milk will not sour. Cooking pots won't boil over. Toast, potatoes, and rice won't burn. The tea and coffee you serve will brew to perfection.

Traditional Kitchen Witches are handcrafted; therefore, no two are the same. They are usually hung from the ceiling, sitting on a broomstick or wooden spoon, which gives such a whimsical illusion that she's flying around, guarding against bad moods and foul foods.

I invite you to make your own Kitchen Witch with a modern twist. Sit her on a pile of pumpkins in the kitchen! Dress her up in high heels and give her a pumpkin purse, a fancy hat and bracelet. Make a Kitchen Witch as original as you are.

Shipwrecked

Last Halloween, a set designer for the movies, who also lives in the neighborhood, decided to save wood scraps all year long for his much anticipated Halloween front yard sensation. And that — it was. He stacked hundreds of pallets into the shape of a wrecked ship, boarded it up and added everything from rope ladders to swampy moss and a mast made from an old telephone pole. Friends helped, other designers added lights, sound effects and transformed junkyard scraps into a spectacular haunted shipwreck for hundreds of Halloween visitors.

Granted, you may not have weeks on end to build an ark, but open up the garage and see what you have. Use old tools tied together to form a tepee shape and put pumpkins all around. Old grapevines make wonderful harvest wreaths. Old sheets, a broomstick, and a ball of newspaper can always become a ghost.

Halloween is gaining popularity as a holiday to celebrate. People are buying loads of decor and treats for the season. They're throwing themed parties and "haunting" the house, sending cards, and sewing costumes for the whole family. Of course, you're encouraged to join in — dress up and take the kids Trick or Treating!

You could send invitations to the big bash at your place this year. You could turn the front yard into a graveyard, cook chili and serve hot apple cider. Whatever you do, the kids will remember... "that one Halloween when Dad dressed up like a pirate and built that huge shipwreck in the front yard..."

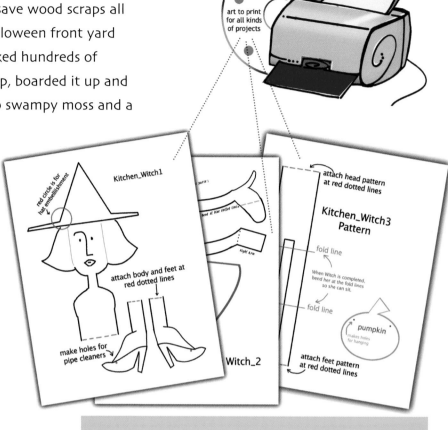

Kitchen Witches (left) are surprisingly easy to make. Print the files Kitchen_Witch1, 2, and 3 from your JennaDisc. Turn to the next page, pull out your tin snips, and get started.

Witch Way? This way

paint her hat with acrylic paint using a foam stencil star for texture

top a feather hair clip with 2 buttons knotted together with burnt orange perle cotton

trace on her face from the pattern, then paint using acrylic paints

paint her pumpkin purse and make the handle from perle cotton

accent her dress with a beaded trim

paint her outfit a bright color hang her dress around her neck

curl up a pipe cleaner with needle nose pliers for shoe pom-poms

3 Kitchen Witches

Materials:

leather work gloves

6' of 8" wide roof flashing

tin snips (scissors for cutting thin metal)

a hammer and nail

fine-grit sandpaper

hot glue

white matte spray paint

acrylic paints

embellishments such as feathers, perle cotton, buttons, pipe cleaners, bead trim, foam stamps

▷ see Resources, page 85.

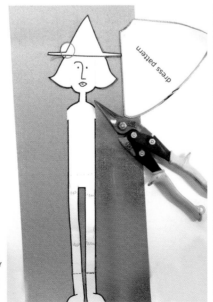 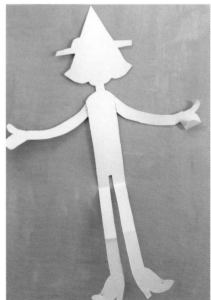

52

Step 1. Print the patterns, Kitchen_Witch1, Kitchen_Witch2, and Kitchen_Witch3 from your JennaDisc. Cut out and tape together as directed on the patterns.

Step 2. Lay clean roof flashing out flat and tape all patterns to flashing. Caution: Tin snips and flashing edges are sharp! Wear work gloves for this project. Cut out witches, dresses, and pumpkins.

Step 3. Make small holes, where indicated on pattern, using a hammer and nail. Sand entire surface of all pieces with fine-grit sandpaper. Spray paint all parts matte white, both sides. Hot glue arms to back of body. Paint witch, dresses, and pumpkins, as you desire. Make her unique! When dry, embellish by painting patterns, gluing bead trim to dresses, etc.

Step 4. Refer to the pattern to bend the witch into sitting position. Bend the hand to hold the purse.

Step 5. Gently arch the dress by hand. Hang dress around her neck by sliding pipe cleaners through the holes at the top of her dress. Make pom-poms on her shoes with pipe cleaners, turning the end of the pipe cleaner with needle nose pliers.

Step 6. String fiber through pumpkin to make handle, knotting in the back. Hang on her hand and welcome in your good Kitchen Witch!

Teachers Deserve More!

...so let's give it to them! Make sweet, spicy and useful gifts for the many special people who guide and give to our children.

Sweet & Spicy

Buy a batch of plain, small jars and fill them with herbs and spices. Print the labels from your JennaDisc and let the kids help stick them to the jars. Tie a ribbon around the top. *See page 93.*

Chalk it up!

Small chalkboards are easy to decorate with colorful papers...and what a perfect gift for a teacher! Print out this modern design from your JennaDisc, cut it into strips wide enough to cover the wooden frame of the chalkboards, and glue it together!

26 End-of-the-Year Teacher's Gifts

Have each child make a chalkboard. Turn the board in the vertical position. Have each child draw a letter of the alphabet until all 26 letters are finished. Attach a ribbon to the back of the frame at the upper right and left hand corners to hang the boards around the classroom. *See page 93 for details.*

54

Recipe Box with a Twist

Print the file **Halloween_3** from your JennaDisc onto photo paper. Everything you need to craft this recipe box is at your fingertips! Turn a plain recipe box into a cheery gift with a twist: Fill it with goodies you can make at home like candies, cookies, or candied nuts. Put them in colored bags and fill the box.

Fancy Candy Pumpkins

Paint a pile of wooden Easter Eggs a warm yellow. Print out retro-chic autumn papers from your JennaDisc and snip the edges until you have a colorful collar for each egg. Fill them with seasonal sweets like candy corn and spiral cookies. *See page 93. Resources, page 85.*

We Be Jammin'

Print jam jar labels onto inkjet sticker paper and attach. Tie a colorful ribbon bow around the neck of the jar and...you'll be jammin'! *See page 93.*

Be the Candy Bag Lady!

Something Sweet to Eat Candy Bags

Make their hum-drum Halloween candy bags something special! Buy gift bags and cover the front with cork. Cut holes for the handles, and you have the perfect place to start creating! Add cute cats, not-too-spooky bats and scare up a whole bunch of candy bags. This is one kind of Bag Lady you'll be proud to be called!

TRICKY! When all the kids have eaten themselves silly and the bag is empty, cut off the front of the bag and use it for scrapbooking. Now, that's what we call a Tricky Treat!

Mad Catter

This friendly feline rules the roost! **Print the files Halloween_1 and Orange_Stripe from your JennaDisc.** Full of cats, text, bats, and icons, you can use these to start your own set of candy bags for the kids. Embellish what comes from the JennaDisc with papyrus papers, a roll of crafter's cork, burlap, sunflower buttons, and more. Use your sewing machine to add texture, hold together layers and give it a folksy feeling. Rip the edges of papers, don't line things up properly, stitch it all with rust colored thread, and before you know it — you'll have them howling for more.

—Dsee Resources, page 85.

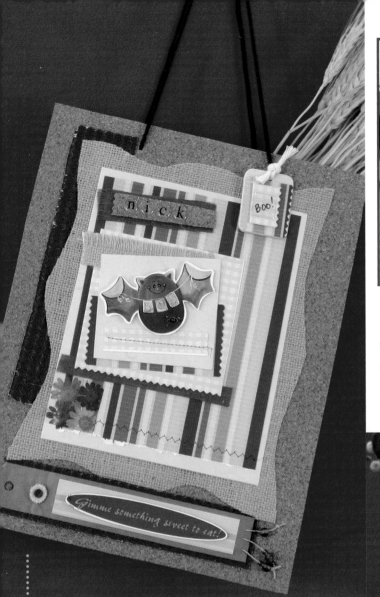

→ Boo! Your **JennaDisc** holds all the art you need to make these Halloween projects. Use the papers for cards, Memory Books, tags, candy bags and more!

Bag Ladies love their printers...

Especially the ones who make Halloween totes with a little help from their JennaDisc. For complete instructions, flip to page 6. You will love using Jenna's art for all your creative endeavors for every season. It's in the Bag!

You've Gone Batty!

Gone Batty? I've always been like this! **Print the files Halloween_1 and Blue_Stripe from your JennaDisc. Use the bats, text, and cats icons to whip up a set of unique candy bags. Embellish images from your JennaDisc with corrugated papers, crafter's cork, twine, dried flower stickers, glass beads, tags and more. Give it a country feeling by sewing together layers and using ripped papers. Do NOT line things up properly. Add wooden tag accents and stitch on accents with rust colored thread.** Call me a dingbat — but Halloween has never looked better.

A Wick in Time

Look at the windfall of autumn designs you can create with some printed tissue paper, candles and hot air. Use berries, wheat and twine to further enhance the seasonal glow. You'll blow them away with this Thanksgiving display of candles — all the patterns are on your JennaDisc.

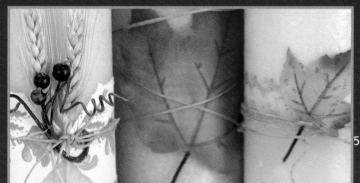

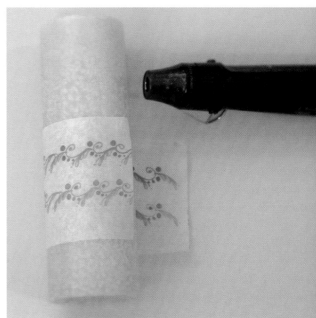

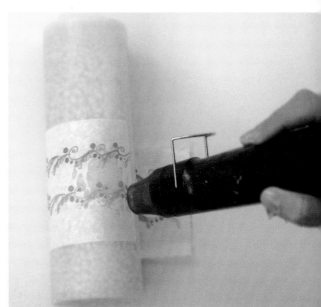

→ **Wick-ed Art!**
Print the JennaDisc files to make these sensational candles.

JennaDisc No.1

art to print for all kinds of projects

→ **Enlighten me!** Use the art from your JennaDisc in a variety of ways such as card making, scrapbooking, gift tags, decoupage boxes, frames, and more. What will you create? Resources, page 85.

Just add heat!

① **Buy** Candles, Tissue Paper, and Freezer Paper. Lightly iron a sheet of tissue paper onto plastic-coated side of freezer paper. ② Cut the paper into 8½" x 11" sheets and use them to print the files **FallBorder_1** and **FallBorder_2**. Remove freezer paper from tissue paper.

③ Cut into the shape or band of pattern you wish. ④ Using a heat gun, heat areas of the candle until just melting, and press the tissue paper onto the wax. Continue melting the wax under the tissue paper for the entire area.

⑤ Embellish as shown (*left*). Hint: try yellow tissue paper.

Wickedly wonderful!

Wintertime

the art of the holiday

It's easy to be absolutely smitten with Wintertime.

It's the time of year for hot cocoa and cold mornings, opening the boxes of Christmas ornaments and closing out the year, the quiet of writing gift lists to the roar of laughter at the table. All of it: the hustle, the hush, too much family, too little time, shopping lists and shoveling snow — it's the time of year I savor. I hope the following pages inspire you use your **JennaDisc** and weave a Winter full of stockings, invitations, memories, and collectibles that will become a cherished part of your traditions.

Merry Making!

There's plenty of Christmas fun afoot with this bright lime and scarlet holiday ensemble. Use your JennaDisc to print out everything you need to make this collection. From the **stocking** pattern to **artwork** for **ceramics** and art for **tags and slippers**, your JennaDisc has it all. Be flamboyant and fun — 'tis the season!

Tag, You're it

Personalize a pile of **gift tags** for all your presents. Print out images from your **JennaDisc** and you'll have plenty of Santas, stripes, pinwheel stripes, 'greetings' text and stockings to assemble a slew of splendid gift tag creations. You will definitely be 'it' with these tags!

→▷See page 67. For JennaDisc instructions, see page 6.

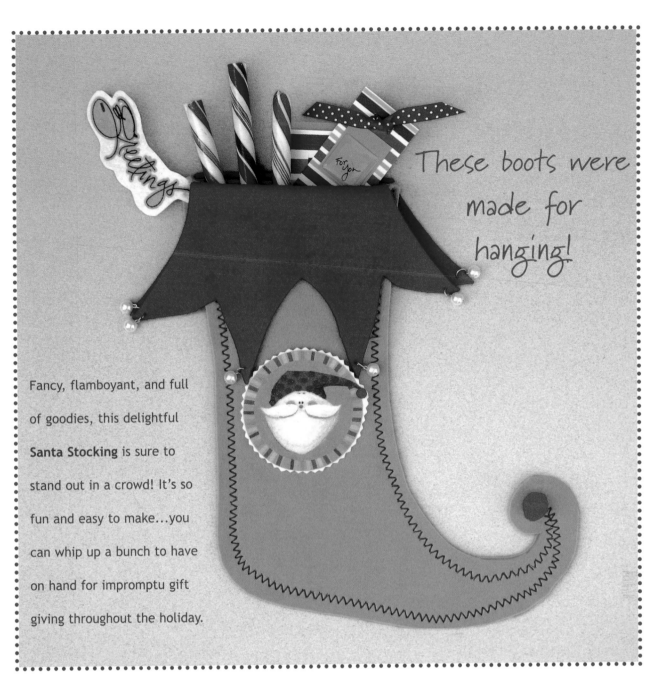

These boots were made for hanging!

Fancy, flamboyant, and full of goodies, this delightful **Santa Stocking** is sure to stand out in a crowd! It's so fun and easy to make...you can whip up a bunch to have on hand for impromptu gift giving throughout the holiday.

Santa Stocking

Materials:

- inkjet iron-on transfer paper (see Resources, pg. 85)
- one 8$\frac{1}{2}$" x 11" sheet of white stiff felt
- $\frac{1}{2}$ yard of green felt
- two 8" x 10" sheets of red felt
- embellishments for the Santa...micro beads, opalescent glitter, and tiny red pom-poms
- white pearls on 7mm jump rings
- fabric glue
- small, fun-shaped hole punch

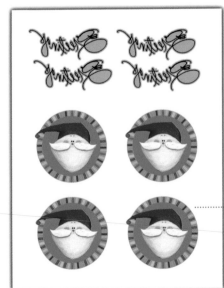

REVERSED! The art on your JennaDisc is even reversed for iron-on transfer so you can read the text.

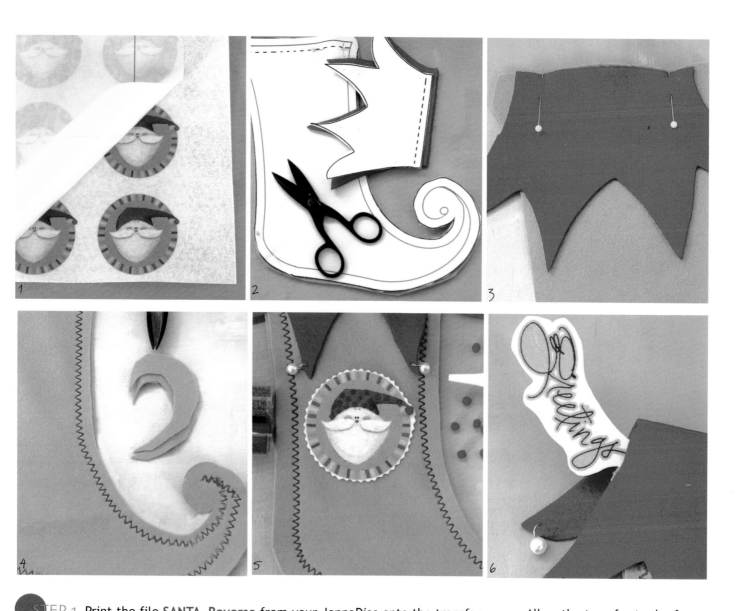

STEP 1. Print the file **SANTA_Reverse** from your JennaDisc onto the transfer paper. Allow the transfer to dry for about 30 minutes. Follow the package instructions to transfer the images onto white stiff felt. For each stocking, use pinking shears to cut out one Santa face.

STEP 2. Print the files Stocking_Pattern1, Stocking_Pattern2 and Stocking_Cuff from your JennaDisc onto white paper. Using the pattern instructions, cut two stockings from green felt and two cuffs from red felt.

STEP 3. Referring to Photo 3, pin one cuff to one stocking piece; sew across the top. Repeat using the remaining pieces to make a stocking side in the reverse direction.

STEP 4. Flipping the cuffs up, match the wrong sides of the stocking pieces together. Zigzag along the edges of the stocking. Carefully trim the excess felt to round the toe (Photo 4). Fold the cuffs down over the stocking. If necessary, trim the stocking edges at each side of the cuff so they don't show.

STEP 5. Embellish the Santa Face as desired. Be creative...use micro beads to make polka dots on his cap, enhance his beard with opalescent glitter, and glue a red pom-pom to the tip of his hat. Glue the Santa to the stocking. Attach the pearls to the tips of the cuff...you can use a tiny hole punch or large needle to make holes for the jump rings to go through.

STEP 6. For the hanger, cut out the word Greetings from the stiff felt (Photo 6). Glue the hanger under the cuff on the left edge of the stocking. Using a hole punch, make a hole for hanging.

Greetings Galore!

This project is a pleaser for the eyes and easy, easy, easy! Use your JennaDisc and print, onto decal paper, all the art you need. Cut out the designs, soak the decal paper in water, and apply to the plates. DONE! Greetings Galore is an understatement!! Handcraft gifts, decorative dishes, pretty plates and bowls for candy. →*For complete instructions, turn to page 94.*

Materials:

- flat white plates, mugs or bowls
- inkjet decal paper
- clear acrylic spray paint or oil-based varnish

→*See Resources, page 85*

All the papers you see here are as far away as your printer. Pop your **JennaDisc** in and press "print." Perfect!

Tag Time Band

Use a plethora of printouts and pile on the accents! Using your **JennaDisc**, you can print out just what you need to make a variety of original tags, cards or scrapbooking pages. **Print the pages, "SANTA1, 2, 3, 4, and 5"** for all your artful needs! For the sampler of gift tags you'll find on page 63, I enhanced my art with many of the products you see on this page: pom-poms, 3-D dots, perle cotton, card stock, vellums, micro beads, and polka dot ribbons. Now, take my art and make your own masterpiece! **Tag, you're it!**

Everyone Loves Cozy Toes!

Step up! These **Santa Slippers** are fun to create! They took about an hour to make — and the hot glue gun did most of the work. Follow the "step-by-step" instructions on the next page and pretty soon you'll be dancing around the house. (Get it?) Give as gifts for the kids, your Mom, the babysitter and your wild Auntie Barb. Foot loose and fancy free has never been easier, especially with your **JennaDisc** in "toe."

→See Resources, page 85

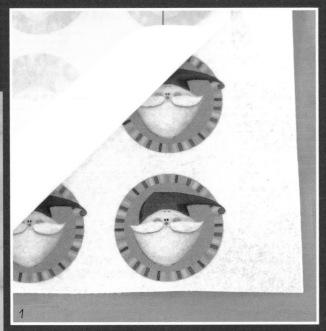

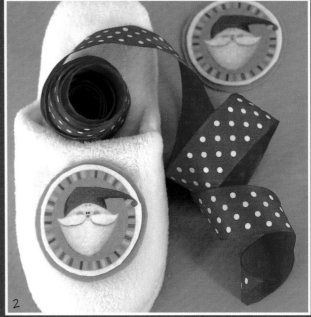

Santa Slippers for Cozy Toes

Materials:

- a pair of terry cloth or velour slippers
- one sheet white stiff felt
- one piece green felt
- iron-on transfer paper
- polka dot wired ribbon, 1" wide

STEP 1. Print, onto inkjet iron-on transfer paper, the file **SANTA_FACES** from your JennaDisc. Iron onto a piece of white stiff felt. Cool and remove paper.

STEP 2. Cut the Santa out leaving a $1/4$" border. Glue it to bright green felt. Use pinking shears or scalloped-edged scissors to cut out $1/4$" around the edge.

STEP 3. Make a bow from wired ribbon.

STEP 4. Hot glue the bow securely to the slipper. Fold the ends of the ribbon under and hot glue them to the sides of the slipper as shown.

STEP 5. Put hot glue on the lower half of the back of the Santa. Press it firmly to the slipper, slightly overlapping the bow. *See photo, opposite page.*

⮕When dry, put on the slippers, turn on your favorite music and dance around a lot. Life is short, shake your booty.

Splendid Snowman is... surprise! a stack of cookie boxes

How could anyone resist this adorable snowman? With whimsical details and a furry white belly, this stacked box set is sure to delight! Using a set of two round jewelry boxes, a bit of ribbon, pom-poms, paint and some imagination, you can create this captivating snowman centerpiece. When he's finished, fill him with cookies and set him out for all to see. He may just be the life of the party!

▷For complete instructions, turn to page 72.

Snappy Sugar Cookies
for all the sweeties on your holiday list

Look too good to eat? No!

May I have one? Sure. These cookies have been printed with edible ink. How fun. And the "paper" they're printed on is cornstarch-based — 100% edible, too. If you have a Canon printer, the edible ink cartridges fit right into your printer. If not, never fear! You can take your JennaDisc to your local bakery. Most bakeries use the Kopykake edible ink system and they will print these designs onto edible cookie forms for a small fee. So use my art and decorate a memorable dessert that's truly good enough to eat!

For this scrumptious plate of sweets, use the Snappy Sugar Cookie recipe on page 87. Frost each cookie with a stiff royal icing. Then, apply the Kopykake printed cookie forms and pipe out more royal icing around the edges.

—▷For more information turn to page 87.

Biscotti Banquet

Cranberry, Macadamia Nut and White Chocolate Biscotti. Bake these beauties for your beloved!

—▷Biscotti recipe, turn to page 94.

A Batch of Beauties!

Biscotti: The Italian coffee cookie made crisp and dry for dunking. Derived from the italian word, biscottio, it means *bis* (twice) and *cotto* (cooked), because each batch gets cooked once in a long slab, then is cooled, sliced, and recooked until crunchy. Traditional biscotti cookies are usually flavored with amaretto or anise seed. Those were the ones my grandfather, an Italian immigrant, used to dip and hold in his morning mug of coffee. After eating the warm, coffee-soaked cookie, he'd ramble lyrical Italian words which could mean nothing short of, "Heaven just rolled past my mouth!"

Today, biscotti are enjoying a revival in a variety of new flavors and combinations guaranteed to thrill your tastebuds. I am especially fond of this recipe (one I augmented from a traditional biscotti recipe) using white chocolate, macadamia nuts and cranberries. Heaven is as close as your kitchen — dunk away!

cookies fur all

make this splendid stacked
cookie box
and fill it with holiday treats!

glue pom-pom to top of hat

stencil paper & make a cone hat

ruffle ribbon with a running
stitch down center

paint box white and add cute
face

below lid, add faux fur

paint cake form with acrylic
red paint

paint wooden balls red and
hot glue them to bottom of tray

cover lid with red paper

make a 1 1/2" wide muffler
from faux fur

make pom-poms, stitch to ends

Wow! That's all there is to say about this
festive stacked cookie box. Fill this Splendid
Snowman with gifts, tasty cookies, or your
favorite holiday treats. Set him out for
all to see — he'll be the coolest part
of the party!

72

1

2

3

4

Splendid Santa Cookie Box

Materials:

- 2 round cardboard boxes, 7" and 5"
- blue metallic paper, 12" x 12"
- red card stock
- 3/4 yard of 1 1/2" wide red satin ribbon
- 1/3 yard faux white sable
- 1 Wilton plastic cake form, 8"
- 4 wooden balls, 1"
- Misc: large pom-pom, glitter, red acrylic paint, aqua yarn for pom-poms
→See Resources, page 85

Detail of photos (*above & right*):

1 Cake Form, balls on skewers to dry and finished cone hat.

2 Finished base. Wooden balls hot glued to base.

3 Fur-covered cookie box & red top.

4 Pom-pom: Notice the needle is threaded with string, not yarn, for added strength.

5 Stencil (*right*) and glitter.

LAST Step: Fill him up! And then, of course, watch it all disappear. That's the idea, right?

73

Paint an Ornamental Christmas!

Turn wooden ornaments into masterpieces with a little help from
Jenna's art. You can turn simple wooden forms into splendid charms and use them for
all kinds of adornments. Trace, paint and celebrate!

Tie your creation on a special
giftbox with ribbons and bows.

Embellish a picture frame
with accents and buttons.

Paint a wooden ornament and
add embellishments!

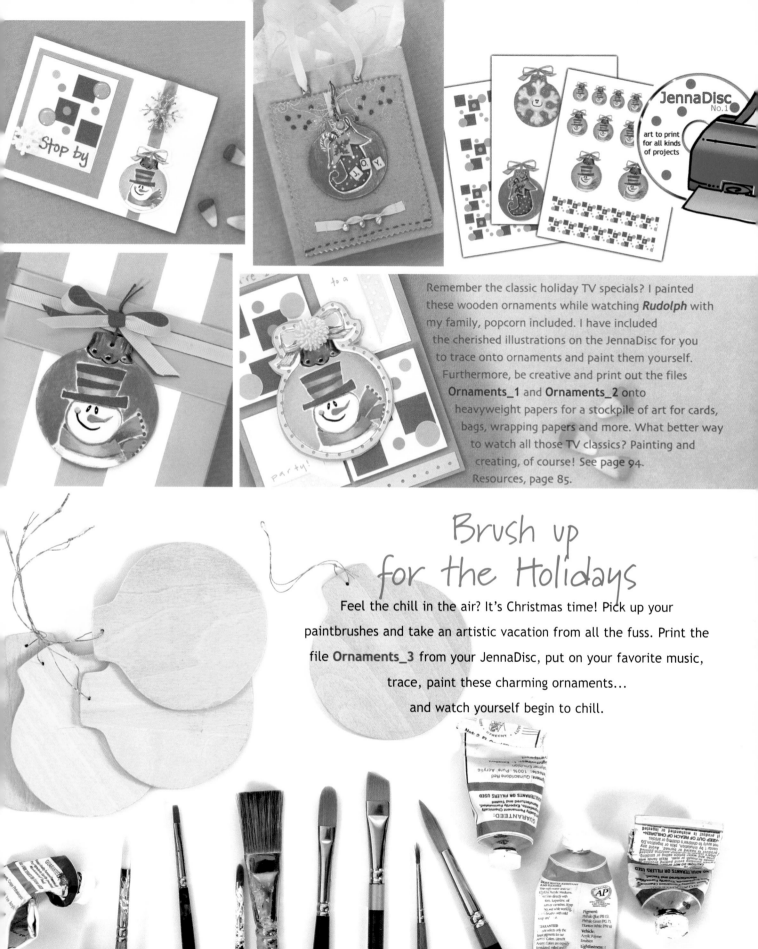

Stop by

Remember the classic holiday TV specials? I painted these wooden ornaments while watching *Rudolph* with my family, popcorn included. I have included the cherished illustrations on the JennaDisc for you to trace onto ornaments and paint them yourself. Furthermore, be creative and print out the files **Ornaments_1** and **Ornaments_2** onto heavyweight papers for a stockpile of art for cards, bags, wrapping papers and more. What better way to watch all those TV classics? Painting and creating, of course! See page 94. Resources, page 85.

Brush up for the Holidays

Feel the chill in the air? It's Christmas time! Pick up your paintbrushes and take an artistic vacation from all the fuss. Print the file **Ornaments_3** from your JennaDisc, put on your favorite music, trace, paint these charming ornaments… and watch yourself begin to chill.

Berry Nice

This bunch of berries deserved a place to be framed! A circle of white linen cardstock was just the thing. The bag is covered with vellum from *Memories in the Making*, a red ribbon runs across the top and green perle cotton is wrapped around the berry bunch. Yes, berry nice.

Brown Baggin' it

A mini bag of grand proportion! Make the tag from scrapbook paper and red embroidery floss. Your JennaDisc has all the words and patterns you need. Get inspired to turn brown bags into terrific gift totes.

Dots Very Festive!

Indeed, they are. Printing out just what you need from your JennaDisc will save you from endless scraps and half-used papers! Print just what you need to make gift bags that might just be better than the gift! Wouldn't this make a great party favor filled with candy canes?

trimmings

Simply Stated

Craft a simple gift bag with a personal touch. Emboss a free-hand drawing of holly onto card stock and use a 3-D adhesive dot to raise it off a vellum tag. Make a pile of these classic gift totes and keep them on hand for last minute gift giving.

Faith

The design works beautifully, frame within frame. On a personal note, this is my favorite bag. I assembled it at a time when I was praying for faith. Trimming the papers, embossing stitches, and gluing artwork together gave me time to hear God's wisdom.

Growing Up on Grosgrain

Grosgrain ribbons were first made in the south of France, and have been a seasonal favorite the world over for centuries. Mix their nostalgic look with some fun text. This art is on your JennaDisc. Top it off with holly berries and a big satin ribbon.

→ Instructions on Page 78
→ Resources on Page 85

all the trimmings

Merry Giftbag

Materials: **"Red Berries"** vellum by Jenna Lynne, red ribbon, green/white striped thread, red satin ribbon, hang tag, 3-D adhesive dots, white linen card stock, paper bag, and JennaDisc art

Cut a tag shape out of white linen card stock. Cover lower space with **"Red Berries"** vellum and cut out icon at the top from the same vellum. Wrap ribbon around top. On photo paper, print the file **Trimmings_1** from your JennaDisc. Cut out the word "Merry" and 3-D adhesive dot it to the front. Punch 2 holes in the tag for the thread.

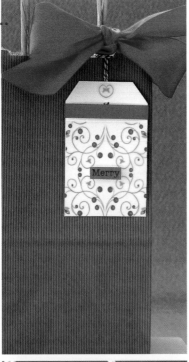

hohoho Giftbag

Materials: small paper bag, scrapbooking paper, striped tag, polka dot grosgrain ribbon, freezer paper, and white cotton fabric

● To prepare fabric to run through your inkjet printer, cut an 8.5" x 11" piece of freezer paper and the same of white cotton. Iron together on waxed side. Put the fabric/paper into the printer, fabric side up. Next, print the file **Trimmings_1** from your JennaDisc onto the fabric. Remove freezer paper. Cut out the words "hohoho" and glue to a striped tag. Hang tag from bag and tie a polka dotted ribbon around top of bag.

Holly Giftbag

Materials: lime green bag, red card stock, and matte inkjet paper

On heavyweight matte paper, print the files **Trimmings_1** and **Trimmings_2** from your JennaDisc. Cut out the holly area and glue it to the bag, leaving the center area unglued. Make the horizontal tag separately from red card stock and Jenna's art. Make 2 slits in the bag for the red tag. Weave the small tag through the slits.

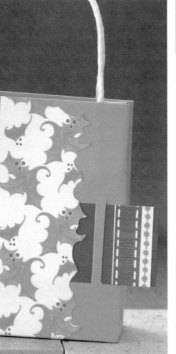

Merry Christmas Giftbag

Materials: white paper bag, freezer paper, white cotton fabric, matte inkjet paper, green scrapbooking eyelets, green seed beads, and thread

On heavyweight matte paper, print the file **Trimmings _1** from your JennaDisc. Cut out the dotted area and glue it to the bag. To prepare fabric to run through your inkjet printer, see ● *above*. Print the file **Trimmings_1** from your JennaDisc onto the fabric. Remove paper. Cut out the words "Merry Christmas" and add eyelets. Glue to the bag. Whip stitch green beads to side of bag.

Your JennaDisc has all these holiday papers ready for you to print and use. No driving to the store for more, no waste, and no waiting. Print Trimmings 1–4 and you'll have art for holiday paper crafts!

78

must-have details

Faith Giftbag

Materials:

white paper bag; green, red & white card stock; inkjet paper; silver & white embossing; eyelets; 3-D adhesive dots; and a silver pen

Cover front section of white bag with red card stock. Onto inkjet matte paper, print the file **Trimmings_3**. Cut the leaf pattern to fit, glue to red card stock. Cut a small red frame of card stock, and emboss white stitches around edges. Emboss the word "faith" onto white gloss card stock, glue to green paper, add eyelets and 3-D mount. Cut out a section of the leaf pattern, edge with silver pen and glue over the word "faith."

Red hohoho Giftbag

Materials:

white paper bag, red berries, satin ribbon, and inkjet paper

Onto inkjet matte paper, print the file **Trimmings_4** from your JennaDisc. Cut pattern to fit the entire front of the bag and glue paper to front. Fold over the top edge twice. Using a hole punch, make 2 holes, 1" apart, in the top of the bag through all layers including the back of the bag. Feed the ribbon through the holes, tie in a bow, and slide some berries behind knot.

Red Berries Giftbag

Materials:

"Red Berries" vellum by Jenna Lynne, white bag, red ribbon, berries, round hang tag, and green perle cotton thread

Cover the front of a gift bag with the **"Red Berries"** vellum. Using a rectangular hole punch, make 2 holes in the center of the bag, and 2 more on each side. Repeat on the back of the bag. Run a red ribbon through the slits all around the bag. Tie a clump of red berries at the stems with green perle cotton. Glue clump to round tag and hang from the center of the bag.

Simply Holly Giftbag

Materials:

white paper bag, silver-edged vellum tag, silver embossing, red and white ribbon, white string, gloss white card stock, and 3-D adhesive dots

Freehand draw some holly leaves and berries onto gloss white card stock with embossing pen. Emboss with silver. Cut out and mount to tag with 3-D dots. Tie tag to the handle with string. Tie a ribbon bow around the bag handle.

Holiday in the City

Modern and bright designs turn the holiday into a glowing success

Bold art, clean lines, and shiny beads turn this Christmas table into a glamorous affair. Make sophisticated votive holders, ornaments, gift boxes, gift tags, and greeting cards in a dramatic theme. Emboss glass ornaments for personalized drama, use candles to add ambiance, and pour some sparkling cider to celebrate the season.

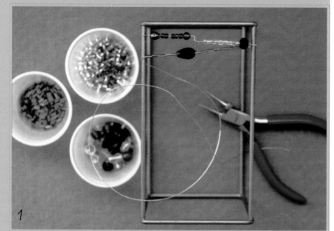

1

All Aglow

Candlelight is the single most important item on a table when ambiance is what you want. Based in a primal urge to surround the campfire, it gives us a sense of comfort and protection. Whatever the reason, candles are undeniably an essential part of every party, so spotlight small votives with this glowing project. These candle holders were covered with a mesh wire when purchased. Simply uncrimp the edge, discard the mesh, and use the metal frame to decorate with beads. The result is a glowing artpiece you can enhance with holiday images from the JennaDisc.

Details: Add One

Choose one theme element and accent it with an opposing texture. If your design element is glass, use glass throughout and add one texture that's very different. Here, I used silk to tie to glass ornaments. It's very soft and balances out the cold edge of the glass.

2

Holiday Votives

Materials:
- votive frame
- white vellum paper
- inkjet transparency paper
- assorted beads
- red micro beads
- 20-gauge gold wire
- small-nosed pliers

STEP 1. Cut six 14" pieces of 20-gauge wire. Wrap one end of the wire securely around the upper corner of votive frame. String on beads, but not enough to fill the space between frame edges. (See photo #1.) Make little crimps along the way between beads. This makes it a piece of art. Cover 2 opposing sides with beads as shown, making crimps. Each side requires approx. 3 wire lengths.

STEP 2. Print the file **Holiday_1** from your JennaDisc onto inkjet transparency paper. Cut 2 large tree images to fit into metal frame openings. Embellish the red dots with red micro beads. Cut 2 vellum pieces of the same size.

3

Details: Eye Candy

Create contrast by repeating the same theme, but in different ways. Try beading other metal shapes, like ornaments and napkin rings. It ties the look together while adding a visual surprise — plus it makes for a conversation opener.

4

STEP 3. With one tree image and one vellum piece together, place eyelets $1/4$" in from the top, on both sides. Secure them to the top of the frame using twisted wire (*shown*). Repeat on opposite side.

STEP 4. Place a small votive inside a glass. When lighting, use caution to keep all flames away from paper. Never leave a burning candle unattended.

→See Resources, page 85.

City Escape

Unfold a glorious holiday with handmade cards and tags

- Onto glossy photo paper, print the files **Holiday_1** and **Holiday_2** from your JennaDisc. Cut out large tree.
- Thread lime green bugle beads around the tree. Cut red and gold ornaments and attach to tree. Add an embossed star.
- Trim the skyline to suit. Use 3-D adhesive dots to attach the tree to card. Fold into 5 sections as shown (*above*).
- Wrap it with a thin gold thread to close (*above left*).

Perfect Papers

Make an unpredictable gift! Top off the best of gifts with a handmade tag. From fancy fibers (fantastic!) to plastic paper clips, surprise everyone with remarkable gift tags. The idea is **artistic composition.** Notice how all three designs (*right*) use an off-center composition. The tree is off to one side, and the "love" focal point (*below right*) is just to the right of center. Use the negative spaces around the focal point to add small points of interest: the silver star tag, the word "peace" in recess, and the skyline add secondary interest. The idea is to have the eye spot the main attraction first, then dance around to the other elements, and return to the main image. Plan your composition before you make the first cuts. Using an off-center style will add that unpredictable element that makes any composition truly artistic.

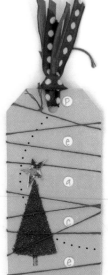

I love the crisp, modern feel of this cityscape. Try printing the designs onto a variety of papers for scrapbooking and wrapping paper. Turn a paper mache box into a stunning gift box (below).

Cityscape Gift Box

Materials: *paper mache round box, inkjet vellum, red glossy paper, white card stock, inkjet glossy photo paper, embossing supplies with gold embossing powder, white acrylic paint, red micro beads and tacky glue.*

Step 1: Print 2 copies of the file **Holiday_2** onto glossy photo paper. Cut to fit the height of the box and wrap the entire lower part of the box. Paint the lid of the box white. Let dry.

Step 2: Cut a 1" strip of the tops of the cityscape design and glue around the lid.

Step 3: Cut and glue a round piece of shiny red paper to the lid. Emboss onto white card stock, using gold, a series of the word "happy" in an area $^1/_2$" smaller than the red circle. Cut circle and glue onto vellum.

Step 4: Print onto inkjet vellum, the file **Holiday_1**. Cut out a tree shape and glue to the top of the embossed words. Embellish the red dots with red micro beads. Emboss a star shape, cut out, and glue to top.

Love to Emboss!

Years ago, as a graphic artist, I learned about embossing for business cards and brochures. It was called thermography. Printing presses were set up with heaters to essentially cook the powder onto the paper, just like embossing. We burned loads of paper at the printers getting the thermography process just right. Last year, my editor, Cyndi, told me about Embossing. Just write or draw onto a surface (like the suspended glass ornament here) with an embossing pen, tap embossing powder on the writing, shake off excess, and heat up the powder with the embossing gun. Watch it bubble up and turn into enamel art! I *LOVE* this!

⟶▷As with all hot instruments, use appropriate caution.
Resources on page 85.

Resources

→▷Unless specified, most items used for crafting and sewing are readily available at your local craft store.

For web shoppers, go to www.**joann**.com, www.**hobbylobby**.com, and www.**michaels**.com.

Art supplies may be available from www.**dickblick**.com.

Specialty fabrics may be available from www.**denverfabrics**.com.

For specific products and specialized crafts, refer to the projects (*below*).

Email Jenna at **create@jennalynne.com**

Trademark and/or copyright symbols may be omitted, but it is understood that all applicable protection laws apply.

Springtime Section

Vintage Valentine

Heart Boxes: All **notions** and **paper mache boxes** from Michaels.
Ribbons from F & S Fabrics, Los Angeles, Jo-Ann Stores, or www.denverfabrics.com.
Pillow: White Inkjet Fabric from June Tailor. www.junetailor.com.
Pillow backing fabric, embroidered wool, from Jo-Ann Stores.

Backpacks

Foam Hearts, item #4622, from Creative Hands, www.fibrecraft.com.
Oil cloth, ball fringe, and notions from www.denverfabrics.com.

Ooolala Pampering Party

Invitation & Place Cards: *Ooolala Papers* and *Suspenders* from Memories in the Making™. Consult your local scrapbooking store for special order if they do not currently carry the line.
Notions from Jo-Ann Stores.
Beaded Bracelet: All supplies from www.firemountaingems.com
Strawberries: Dolci Frutta, at local grocery store. www.sacfoods.com
Place Mat: Dupioni silk and beaded trim from specialty fabric store. Mountain Mist Polyester Quilt Batting from Michaels.
Napkin Ring: Cost Plus Imports
Towels: Target Stores. Notions from Jo-Ann Stores.
Canvas Frames: Aaron Brothers. **Inkjet Canvas** from Strathmore.

Ooolala Sandals: Designed by Jenna Lynne for Time & Again™. Go to www.Ganz.com.

Extravagant

Waxmelter Batik Pen, X-fine tip, Rabinowitz Design Workshop, (203) 393-2397, 8 Carmel Road, Bethany, CT 06524. Hobby Lobby may carry a non-electric version, or try www.surmastore.com. **Glass Plates, Vase and Napkin Rings** from Cost Plus Imports.
Lazertran Decals, see page 86.

Eggspress Yourself

Artist Inkjet Papers by Strathmore, WEAVE #59761, from www.dickblick.com. Card papers from scrapbooking store.

Zen & Now

Artist Inkjet Papers by Strathmore, WEAVE #59761 and TEXTURE #59701, from www.dickblick.com. **Inkjet papers** from Epson, Heavyweight Matte. www.epson. com. **Metal Embellishments** from Memories in the Making™, Leisure Arts, specialty scrapbooking stores.
Tray, box and papers from Michaels.

Summertime Section

Patriotic Party

Everything used was purchased at a craft/hobby store.
Boats: Darice®Wood Model Kit, Titanic.
Rise to the Occasion Cake Riser: Riser from Michaels Stores.
Hanging Stars from Midwest of Cannon Falls, purchased at a fabric store. www.midwestofcannonfalls.com
Coasters: Cost Plus Market
Seeing Stars Watermelon Centerpiece: Flowerpot from craft store. **Star-shaped cookie cutter** from Sur La Table, Item #1677. www.surlatable.com. **Nautical Glass decorations** are from Nautica. Additional decorations from craft store.

Old Glory Days

Scrapbooking papers and embellishments from specialty scrapbooking stores. **Inkjet papers** from Epson, Heavyweight Matte. www.epson. com.
Inkjet fabric from June Tailor, craft stores. www. junetailor. com
5" x 7" Memory Book from Kolo.

Beach Babes

Tray from Jo-Ann Stores Fabric store. **Soap Dispenser, Cups, Ice Bucket** from Target Stores, Gina brand. **Hats** from Cherokee and Jo-Ann Stores. **Onesies** and **Bibs** from Carter's, Target stores. **Lazertran Decals**, see page 86. **Beach Babes Memory Frame:** Aaron Brother's 12" x 12" scrapbooking frame. **Knobs from** Michaels stores. **Photo paper and inks** from Epson.

What's Cookin', Dad?

Apron from craft store. **Inkjet fabric** from June Tailor, craft stores. www.junetailor.com. Additional items: ribbons, buttons, etc., from fabric store. **CD cases:** Plain Jane CD pouches, www.twinsisters.com. **Invitation:** specialty scrapbooking stores for papers. **Inkjet papers** from Epson, Heavyweight Matte. www.epson.com.

Autumn Section

Falling on Card Times

Papers from www.Dick Blick.com or art store. **Inkjet papers** from Epson, Heavyweight Matte, www.epson.com. Additional items: ribbons, buttons, etc., from scrapbooking store.

What a Witch!

Roof Flashing, tin snips, sand paper, from the local hardware store. Additional items: rickrack, ribbons, paints, buttons, etc., from craft store. **Bead trim** from Decorative Details, Jo-Ann Stores.

Teachers Deserve More

Glass spice bottle in a 6 pack, from Cost Plus Imports. **Glass jam jars, chalkboards and embellishments** from Michaels. **Inkjet full-sheet adhesive label paper** from Avery, Office Depot. **Inkjet papers** from Epson, Heavyweight Matte. www.epson. com.

Wintertime Section

Making Merry/Greetings Galore

Plates, Serving Tray, Cups, Bowls from Pier 1 Imports and Cost Plus Imports. **Inkjet Decal papers** from Lazertran. See page 86. www.lazertran.com. **Krystal Kote Acrylic Spray Paint**, Michaels. Additional items: ribbons, buttons, etc., from scrapbooking store.

Santa Stocking

Inkjet iron-on Transfer Paper, from June Tailor. **Stiff felt, felt fabrics, pearls** from Jo-Ann Stores store. **Embellishments**, Michaels.

Tag, You're it

Inkjet papers from Epson, Heavyweight Matte. www.epson. com. Additional items: microbeads, buttons, etc., from scrapbooking store.

Everyone Loves Cozy Toes Slippers

Slippers from Bed, Bath & Beyond. **Wired Ribbon** from F & S Fabrics, Los Angeles, also try www.denverfabrics.com or Jo-Ann Stores. **Inkjet iron-on Transfer Paper,** from June Tailor. **Stiff felt** and **felt fabrics** from Jo-Ann Stores.

Splendid Snowman

Round Jewelry Boxes from Revelations™ www.ericas.com or gift stores. **Papers** from scrapbooking store. **Faux Fur (Ranch Mink, White)** www.big4fabrics.com/fakefur. **Ribbon** from Jo-Ann Stores. **Yarn** for muffler from Reynolds™, color #133, Utopia, Jo-Ann Stores. **All other supplies**, Michaels.

Ornamental Christmas

Wooden Ornaments, paper mache picture frame, paints, bags, embellishments from Michaels stores. **Snowflake embellishments** and **large striped paper** from Memories in the Making™. Consult your local scrapbooking store for special order if they do not currently carry the Ooolala Line. **Scrabble® Letter Stickers,** Target stores.

All the Trimmings

Red Berries Christmas scrapbooking paper from Memories in the Making™. Consult your local scrapbooking store for special order if they do not currently carry the line (Jenna's Christmas Line).

Holiday in the City

Inkjet papers from Epson, Photo Paper. www.epson.com. **Inkjet transparency paper** from Office Depot. Votive Frame, wire, beads, pliers, gift boxes, embellishments from Jo-Ann Stores. **Embossing materials** from Michaels.

Lazertran

Lazertran inkjet decal paper is designed to be used with any printer that uses ink. It is not designed for toner-based machines. The surface of the inkjet paper is absorbent and will only take a small amount of ink. If too much ink is applied then the image will bleed. Find a setting on your inkjet printer that applies as little ink as possible. Plain paper setting is generally acceptable.

STEP 1. Put a sheet of Lazertran Inkjet paper into your printer and print onto the smooth, creamy, white side. The backside of the paper is a light greenish-blue.

STEP 2. Print your image and allow to dry for 1 hour. In this time the inks will become waterproof.

STEP 3. Soak in warm water for a minute or so and the image will be released on a decal. Note: The decal will dry white where there is no color.

STEP 4. If you want the decal to be clear/translucent, spray it with a clear acrylic gloss paint. Try **Aervoe Interior/Exterior High Gloss Coat or Plasti-Kote Fast Dry Enamel.** Make sure the whole image is penetrated with varnish and free of bubbles. Be careful to apply the spray in fine mists and gradually build up the coating to avoid destroying the decal.

TIPS: Choose your plates/mug/bowl carefully. A flat surface is paramount. The decal paper does not stretch or mold to curves or bumps. Therefore, pick simple, flat shaped ceramics.

• Before putting the decal in water, lay it out on the ceramic piece and trim all edges to size, cutting decal as close to the actual size as needed. Once wet, use caution to not rip the decal.

Plates are for decorative purposes and not dishwasher safe.

Go to **www.lazertran.com** to learn more.

Spring Pleaser Plates
from page 22.

<u>Large plates:</u> Print onto Decal paper (*below*) the file Citrina11x17. Your inkjet printer must accommodate 11"x17 "paper or larger. If not, your local copy shop can do the job. Make sure you specify INKJET when printing.

<u>7" square plates:</u> Print onto Decal paper the file Citrina7x7. Trim to size and follow decal instructions (*left*).

Next, turn the plates upside down and set on a jar or bowl. Place the decal on the **underside of the eating surface.** Once dry, if the plate has blunt edges, run masking tape around the edges. With the plate still upside down, use **satin finish spray paint** and lightly coat the plates. Let dry between coats. Apply 3 coats of paint. Remove masking tape. Coat with one coat of **clear varnish spray paint.**

* These plates are best used as decorative serving plates. Granted, they are well sealed with varnish, but wash gently and dry by hand immediately.

High Seas Coasters from page 37.
Print onto Decal paper the file 4thBigStars. Follow Lazertran directions (*left*). When dry, finish the project by spraying with clear acrylic spray paint.

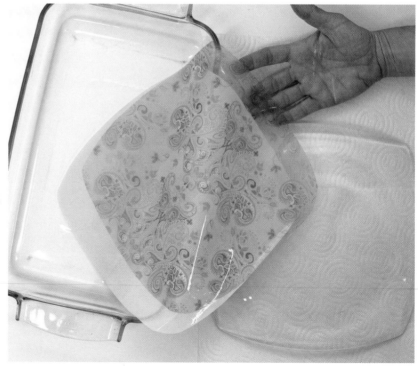

Kopykake

Kopykake inkjet cake & cookie decorating papers and inks are edible. They are designed to be used with Canon printers. If you do not have a Canon printer, your local bakery most likely has this entire system and will charge you a small fee to print the designs from your JennaDisc onto cookies and papers.

If you have a Canon Printer: Replace your regular printer inks with Kopykake Edible Inks and replace your regular paper with Kopykake Edible Frosting Sheets then use your current equipment to produce designs for your cookies and cakes. If you need design software then simply download the "Desktop Decorator" at **www.kopykake.com**.

Valentine's Day Cookies
from page 18.
Kopykake makes a variety of edible cookie forms for decorating. From circles to hearts and more, these edible forms are ready for inkjet printing with edible inks or to draw on with edible ink pens. Read details above. For this project, heart-shaped forms were used with edible ink pens.

Splendid Snowman Snappy Sugar Cookies
from page 71.
Read Kopykake (*above*). Print the file **Splendid_Cookies** from your JennaDisc following the instructions above and place cookie forms on frosted cookies. Pipe frosting around the edges of the cookies and sprinkle with sugar or coconut flakes. Serve within 6 hours.

Snappy Sugar Cookies

$1/2$ cup butter or margarine, softened
1 cup granulated sugar
1 egg
1 1/2 teaspoons vanilla extract
1/2 teaspoon almond extract
2 cups all-purpose flour
1/2 teaspoon baking powder
1/4 teaspoon salt

Cream butter and sugar until light and fluffy. Beat in egg and extracts. Sift together dry ingredients. Gradually add dry ingredients to creamed mixture, blending well. Wrap dough in plastic wrap and chill at least 1 hour. On a lightly floured surface, use a floured rolling pin to roll out dough to 1/8" thickness. Cut out dough using desired cookie cutters. Place cookies on lightly greased baking sheets.

Preheat oven to 400°. Bake 8-10 minutes or until edges are lightly browned. Remove from sheets and cool on wire racks.

Yield: approximately 3 dozen cookies

Materials: 12" of black trim with loops, pink ribbon $^3/_{16}$" wide, 2 pink dot crystals 5mm, Glue Stick™, all papers are Ooolala Papers, Ooolala stickers.™ —▷See Resources, Page 84.

Step 1: SLIDING INSERT. Using Ooolala scrapbooking papers and stickers, make a 2" wide pull with $^1/_4$" notches at the bottom. Write a personalization on it, either by hand or using a graphics program. Add pink dot crystals as shown (fig. 1).

Step 2: CARD FRONT & FLAP. Using mint green cardstock, cut a piece 12" x 7". Score and fold at 3" from the left and again at $7^1/_2$" from the left. Cover the front flap with scrolled paper. Cut curly edges freehand along the scrolls of the paper.

Step 3: INNER FRONT FLAP WITH SLIDER. Cut a $3^3/_4$" x $6^1/_4$" high piece of pink cardstock. Scallop cut right and left sides. Make a slit $1^1/_2$" from the top, $^1/_4$" from the left, 2" wide. Put slider through slit. Glue only edges of pink piece to inner flap of card, so slider can move. Glue 2 strips of black trim to the flaps to make corset.

Step 4: INSIDE OF CARD. Onto pink cardstock, print **talk_1** from your JennaDisc. Cut to size, add Ooolala Girl sticker. Onto mint cardstock, print **talk2** from your JennaDisc. Cut **talk2** down to $2^1/_2$" wide, $3^1/_2$" high. Write party particulars by hand.

PARTY DOME: Cut a square piece of pink paper to fit a clear acrylic self-adhesive dome. Stick the word "Party" from Ooolala stickers to pink paper. Stick dome to top. Glue to top edge of **talk2** slider. Cut proper sizes of green scrolled transparency for both right and left sides of card. Make a slit for the **talk2** slider and glue both transparencies to edges only.

Step 5: When the card is all ready to send, thread the ribbon up from the bottom of the corset to the top, criss crossing as you go.

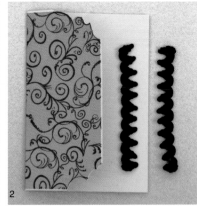

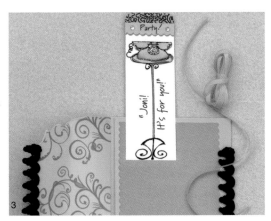

Napkin Ring & Place Mat, from page 26.

Materials for Napkin Ring:
chain nose pliers
7mm jump rings
assorted large beads
scrolled napkin ring, see Resources, page 84.

Steps: Using chain nose pliers, open 7mm jump rings. Add large shiny beads to jump rings and close onto scrolls of napkin ring

Materials for Place Mat:
$^1/_2$ yard dupioni silk
12" x 18" piece of batting
black bead trim
12mm black beads.

Steps: Cut 2 pieces of dupioni silk, 13" x 19". Cut 2 pieces of black beaded trim, 13" long. With right sides together, place bead trim in between fabric layers, beads facing inward. Stitch around both beaded sides and top. Turn inside out; press. Slide batting into place mat. Press lower section edges under and stitch closed by hand. Stitch black beads in a diamond pattern, pulling stitch through entire place mat for tufted effect.

Beaded Beauty Bracelet, from page 27.

Materials: See Resources, page 84.

7 to $7^{1}/_{2}''$ silver-plated bracelet w/lobster claw clasps

2 chain nose pliers

70 silver-plated jump rings, size 6mm

Beads: 4 colors of your choice, size 6. Around 5 grams total. Shown: 50% triangle beads in light and dark pink, 25% round silver beads, 25% round silver/black beads

● **BEAD JUMP RINGS.** Open a jump ring with pliers in both hands; pull the left hand toward you, the right hand rotating away. Put 3 beads on each jump ring. Still holding with pliers, slide the open jump ring onto the first link of the bracelet, then close jump ring with pliers (right hand moves toward you, the left hand rotates forward). Repeat this process putting 2-3 beaded rings onto each link.

● **Charm at end of bracelet:** Link 4 plain jump rings together like a chain. On the single final jump ring, add 6 beaded jump rings. Using a jump ring, attach the opposite end of the charm chain to the end of the bracelet, so it dangles when the bracelet is latched.

Eggsuberant

from page 24.

Materials:

glue stick
lime green, pink, yellow, and orange cardstock
Strathmore™ inkjet weave paper or other textured inkjet paper (See Resources, page 84)
deckle-edge craft scissors

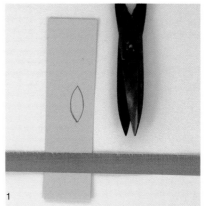

Step 1: For the flower center, cut a 6" by $^{1}/_{2}$" long piece of orange cardstock. Draw a line down the center, horizontally. Make tiny clips along one edge, just to the line. For the flower stabilizer, cut three 1" long, leaf-shaped pieces from green cardstock.

Step 2: Apply glue along the unclipped edge of the flower center. Tightly role the paper and securely glue the end. Gently spread the flower center open.

Step 3: From your JennaDisc, print the file, **Spring_Flower** onto texturized inkjet paper. Cut out both the base flower and the upper petals. Insert the flower center through the holes. Fold the 3 stabilizers in half and glue the top half to the bottom sides of the flower center.

Step 4: Make a 5" square card from lime green cardstock. Print the **Citrina2** paper from your JennaDisc onto texturized paper. Cut a 5" square from the Citrina paper...cut a $^{5}/_{8}$"w frame from the square. Use the deckle-edge scissors to cut a $3^{1}/_{2}$" square from yellow cardstock. Glue the frame and the yellow square to the card.

Step 5: Attach the flower to the card by gluing the bottom half of the stabilizers to the card; press firmly.

FROM SEA TO SHINING SEA

U.S.S. Dad

5

Nautical Place Card Boats

from page 37.

Materials:

$7^{1}/_{4}$" x 2" Wood Titanic Model Kit
(you will only use the boat)
white spray paint
black paint pen
red and blue acrylic paint
masking tape
one $^{5}/_{8}$" dia. wooden ball
two $^{5}/_{16}$" dia. wooden balls
36" long, $^{3}/_{16}$" dia. wooden dowel
white inkjet canvas
12" square of white cotton or linen
fabric
toothpicks
cotton string
wood glue
craft glue
craft drill with $^{3}/_{16}$" dia. bit

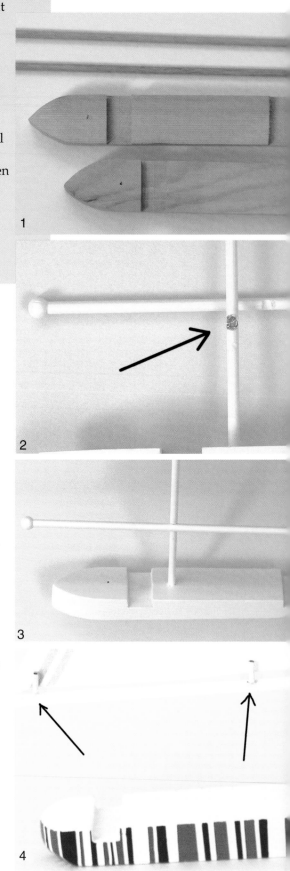

1

2

3

4

○ Allow paints to dry after each application.

○ Step 1. Paint the base of the boat white; allow to dry. Use the paint pen to write the name on the boat (fig. 1).

○ Step 2. For the red stripes, apply vertical pieces of masking tape around the edge of the boat...vary the distance between the pieces of tape to make wider and thinner lines. Paint the areas between the pieces of tape red; allow to dry. Carefully remove the tape and repeat to make the blue lines.

○ Step 3. Cut two 8 $^{1}/_{2}$" pieces of dowel. For the mast, carefully cut a notch in one dowel 6" from one end...this will hold the boom dowel in place. Spray paint the dowels, balls, and several toothpicks white. Use the craft drill to enlarge the mast hole in the boat to $^{3}/_{16}$". If necessary, enlarge the holes in the balls to $^{3}/_{16}$" to fit the dowels (fig. 2).

○ Step 4: Glue the boom in the notch of the mast with one end 5" from the notch. Wrap the intersection with string in an "x" and tie the ends to secure (fig. 3). Glue the large ball to the top of the mast and the small balls on each end of the boom.

○ Step 5. Cut or break four $^{1}/_{4}$"-long pieces from the toothpicks. Using wood glue, attach them at a 90-degree angle to the back mast and boom (fig. 4). Allow to dry.

○ Step 6: For the main sail, print the **4thSails** file from your JennaDisc onto inkjet canvas. Cut out the sail and remove the paper. Cut a 6" x 3$^{1}/_{2}$"w right triangle from white fabric for the jib sail. Glue the main sail to the toothpicks and the jib directly to the mast and boom (fig. 5); trim the top point from the jib. Tie a length of string around the jib end of the boom, then secure the opposite end at the mast and boom intersection.

○ Step 7. For the deck rope, cut a 12" piece of string; knot one end. Mix a small amount of 1 part craft glue to 1 part water. Dip the rope in the mixture and remove the excess. Beginning with the unknotted end, wrap the rope in a coil; allow to dry. Glue the rope to the deck of the boat.

What's Cookin', Dad? from page 44.

Apron: Materials: white inkjet fusible fabric, red and yellow embroidery thread, 4 red buttons, 2 yellow buttons, 2 yds. of 1" wide blue grosgrain ribbon, white apron, Fabri-Tac™ Glue. Print the files **BBQ_1** and **BBQ_3** from your JennaDisc onto fusible inkjet fabric. Cut out the square image from **BBQ_1**, leaving ¼" of white edge around image. Set aside. Taking the blue ribbon, make a square by darting the ribbon on the edges to make a 90 degree angle. The square of ribbon should be ½" wider than the square image. Glue the ribbon to square. When dry, iron (fuse) the square image and ribbon to apron. Sew 4 red buttons to the corners with embroidery thread. Cut out the words, "What's Cookin'?" from **BBQ_3** and the strip that runs across the top of the apron, iron to apron. Sew 2 yellow buttons to the corners. For the neck cord, cut a length of ribbon 1" longer than the neck cord, folding ends under by ½". Fold the ribbon in half, covering the white apron cord. Sew the edge of the ribbon over the cord.

CD case: Materials: blank CD case, matte heavyweight inkjet paper, scrapbooking papers and supplies like deckle-edged scissors and 3-D adhesive dots.
Print the file, **BBQ_2** from your JennaDisc onto matte inkjet paper and assemble the case as shown (*below*).

Invitation: Materials: matte heavyweight inkjet paper, scrapbooking papers and supplies like deckle-edged scissors and 3-D adhesive dots.
From the JennaDisc, print the files, **BBQ_1, BBQ_3,** and **BBQ_4** onto either photo paper or heavyweight matte paper. Make an folder-style envelope from shiny red coated cardstock. Add icons from **BBQ_3** and freehand write, #1 Dad. Make insert by printing the file **BBQ_4** and writing in the information, either by hand or using a graphics program. Mount onto royal blue cardstock. Cut out icons and use 3-D adhesive dots to apply.

Watermelon Flower Arrangement

from page 37. Materials: flower pot, iceberg lettuce, kale, watermelon, strawberries, wooden skewers, toothpicks, and decorative accents. Using a star-shaped cookie cutter, make stars from watermelon and slide onto skewers. Slide strawberries on skewers. Fill base of flowerpot with iceberg lettuce, cover with kale, and hold with toothpicks. Gently push skewers with fruit into lettuce. Add decorative touches like mylar toothpicks and nautical glass stirring rods. Eat within an hour of assembly.

Beach Babes from page 40.

Hats: Materials: white inkjet fusible fabric from June Tailor, embroidery thread, 2 buttons per hat, tiny hole punch.
● STEP 1. Using a text layout program, write the name you wish in a bold, fun font, approx. 2½" high. Print out the name and cut out each letter.
● STEP 2. Print the file(s) **Beach_Blue** or **Beach_Pink** from your JennaDisc onto white inkjet fabric. Pin the letters to the fabric and cut out each letter.
● STEP 3. Using a tiny hole punch, make holes at the top of each letter. Cut a piece of embroidery thread at least 6" longer needed and thread the letters on using a needle. When completed, press the needle through the hat and tie off. Take the needle and thread it to the other end of the thread and press through the hat and tie off, leaving the thread a bit of loose.
● STEP 4. Iron the letters to the hat, leaving a bit of slack thread between letters for style.

Tray, Bucket, Cups, Suntan Lotion Dispenser
from page 40-41.

Materials: Lazertan inkjet decal paper, various PLASTIC trays, soap dispensers and cups. See Resources, page 85.
Tray: Your printer must accommodate paper 11"x17" papers. If not, your local copy shop can provide an oversized inkjet printer. Print Beach_Babes11x17 from your JennaDisc and follow the Lazertran directions on page 86. Apply the decal to the underside of the tray. **When finished applying the inkjet decals, spray the images with clear gloss varnish spray paint. Cups, etc.:** Print Beach_Blue or Beach_Pink and Beach_Suntan onto decal paper. See Tray directions, *above.* Spray with clear gloss varnish.
Bibs and Onesies: Print Beach_Blue or Beach_Pink and Beach_Suntan onto colorfast fusible inkjet fabric from June Tailor. Cut out icons and iron on following package directions.

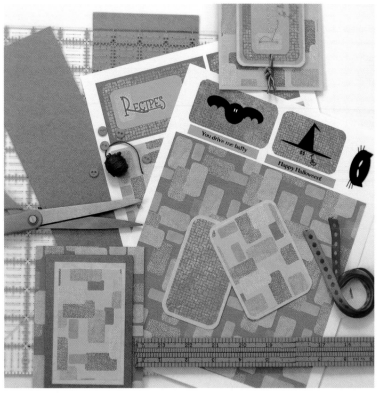

Falling on Card Times
from page 48.

Materials, see page 49. To assemble cards, print the files, **Halloween_2** and **Halloween_3** onto either heavy-weight matte paper or photo paper. Hint: Use a scrapbookers corner-punch to make rounded corners.

Drive Me Batty: Cut out the bat image. Around the edge, draw a squiggly black line with permanent marker. Glue bat rectangle to background print; cut out. Cut out "You drive me batty" making sure to leave both horizontal edges wide enough to put place eyelets. Add eyelets. Glue at an angle to bat rectangle. Glue rectangle to yellow cardstock, trimming to leave a $^1/_4$" border. Repeat onto bronze scrapbooking paper. Set aside. Cover the front of a 4" x 6" card with background print. Mount bat image to card with 3-D adhesive dots.

Be Catty: Cut out the cat image. Around the edge, draw a squiggly black line with permanent marker. Cut out "Happy Halloween!" making sure to leave both horizontal edges wide enough to put place buttons. Thread bronze colored perle cotton through 2 small orange buttons and knot. Glue to "Happy Halloween!" Glue to bronze paper, trim straight on top and side edges, deckle-edge cut the bottom. Cover a playing card with yellow card stock. Trim background paper $^1/_4$" smaller than yellow block and attach with glue. Cover the front of a 4" x 6" card with bronze paper and dry-brush paint with copper acrylic paint. Glue playing card to 4" x 6" card. Mount cat image and borders to playing card with 3-D adhesive dots.

Pumpkin Face: Cut a pumpkin-shaped piece of orange fiber paper and glue to white cardstock. Add a green paper pumpkin stem. With permanent marker, draw on a happy pumpkin face. Trim, leaving a white border. Cover a playing card with yellow card stock. Trim edges off with deckle-edged scissors. Cut out the small tile-like rectangle from papers. Glue to yellow card. Glue pumpkin to rectangles. Using a rectangular hole punch, make a hole in the left side of the

rectangle and tie a ribbon through the hole. Set aside. Cover the front of a 4" x 6" card with yellow cardstock. Cut a 3 $^1/_4$" x 5 $^1/_4$" piece of yellow background pattern; glue background to 4" x 6" card. Mount playing card to 4" x 6" card with 3-D adhesive dots.

Happy Spells: Cut out the witch image. Mount onto white card stock; decal-edge cut the edges. Mount onto a rectangular piece of balsa wood. Set aside. Cut out the rectangle shaped tile pattern. Mount onto yellow card stock and trim, leaving a border. Cover the front of a 4" x 6" card with yellow cardstock and glue yellow rectangle to card in vertical position. Glue a red ribbon across card. Tie a knot of bronze perle cotton through 2 orange buttons. Glue in place. Paint a small wooden sign butter yellow. When dry, write "Happy Spells 5¢" as shown. Knot fibers around sign handle. Glue to rectangle. Glue witch block to card front.

Teachers Deserve More from page 54.

Materials: various glass spice bottles, jam jars, wooden recipes boxes, wooden egg-shaped baskets, chalkboards, ribbons, butter yellow acrylic paint. Papers: jam jars and spice bottles require Avery™ inkjet label paper. Other paper projects require heavyweight matte inkjet paper or photo paper.

Spice bottles & jam jars: Print the files, **Jars_1** and **Jam_1** onto inkjet label paper. Cut out shapes and adhere to jars. Tie on ribbons and write on labels.

Chalkboards: Paint the wooden area of the chalkboard butter yellow. Print the file **Halloween_2** and cut strips to cover the frame of the chalkboard.

Card: Print the file **Halloween_3** and make a greeting card as shown.

Wooden egg-shaped baskets: Paint wooden basket area yellow. Print the file **Halloween_3** and cut strips approximately 1" wide, using a scalloped-edge scissor for the lower edge. Cut snips in the paper, from the top of the paper to within $^1/_4$" of the lower edge. Glue to the eggs.

Gifted Labels

Print the files **Jars_1** and **Jam_1** for a kitchen full of matching spice jars and jams. Great gifts for an orderly kitchen!

Beach Babes Memory Frame! from page 42.

Print the files **Beach_Big_Blue** or **Beach_Big_Pink** as a background paper onto Photo paper. These over-sized files need a printer that accommodate papers as large as 11" x 17." The page you are creating will be 10.75" x 10.75."

Print the files **Beach_Suntan** and **Beach_Blue** or **Beach_Pink** onto letter-sized papers for the icons and images. Use a graphics program or write journaling by hand. Remember, the frame will require a 2-dimensional image. The use of any 3-D embellishments will not work. Mount your finished work onto a 12" x 12" piece of heavy scrapbooking paper. Set in frame. Glue 2 wooden knobs, painted to match, to the outside of the frame for towel holders.

What a wonderful gift for (or from) grandparents!

Biscotti Banquet, from page 71.
Cranberry and White Chocolate Biscotti

¹/₂ cup fresh cranberries, finely chopped

³/₄ cups dried sweetened cranberries

³/₄ cups macadamia nuts or almonds

2 cups all-purpose flour

1/2 tsp. cinnamon

2 tsp. baking powder

1 cup sugar

¹/₃ cup butter or margarine, softened

2 eggs

white chocolate chips

red chocolate pieces

Preheat oven to 375°. In a bowl, cream butter and eggs. Add the rest of the ingredients, except chocolate. Stir just until the mixture is combined. Divide the dough into 2 loaves. Place on greased cookie sheets. Each loaf should be about 8 inches long and 3 inches wide. Bake for 25-30 minutes or until a toothpick inserted in the center comes out clean. Cool for 1 hour. Cut each loaf diagonally into ³/₄" thick slices on cookie sheet. At 300°, bake for 20 minutes, then turn over and bake for 25 minutes more until crisp. Transfer to wire racks to cool.

To drizzle the biscotti with chocolate, put a handful of white chocolate chips in a gallon-sized freezer bag; close with a loose rubber band. Set it, chips down, into a glass measuring cup. Microwave on low for a minute. Remove and squeeze the bag to see how melted chips are. Continue to microwave until just soft enough to drizzle. (Do not overheat chocolate; it will burn.) Cut away a tiny piece of the corner of the bag and squeeze out the warm chocolate. Repeat again with the red chocolate pieces.

Lastly, no biscotti is any good without a cappuccino. I'm Italian — that's just the way it is — so froth up some milk, pour it in your coffee and sip, and dip, your way to a bit of heaven!

Greetings Galore, from page 66.

For detailed instructions on how to use inkjet decal papers, go to page 86. Choose your plates/mug/bowl carefully. A flat surface is paramount. The decal you will be transferring does not stretch or mold to curves or bumps. Therefore, pick simple, flat shaped ceramics.

7" Plates: Print the files **SANTA1** and **SANTA2** from the JennaDisc onto Lazertran inkjet decal paper. When completed, spray the plates with a clear acrylic spray such as Krystal Klear™ or an oil-based varnish.

Trays, Mugs, Bowls, Vases, etc. Print the following files from your JennaDisc; **SANTA_FACES**, **SANTA3**, and **SANTA4**. Cut stripes, Santa faces, greetings and icons of all sizes to decorate all sorts of white bowls, plates and cups. When completed, spray the items with a clear acrylic spray such as Krystal Klear™ or an oil-based varnish. Fill with red carnations, candies, or gifts. Hang from the wall and hearth. Create collections for greater impact, keeping all the plates white. Personalize the plates with ceramic paint pens as a special gift.

Ornamental Christmas, from page 74.

Frame: Print the file **Ornaments_3**. Trace image onto wooden ornament. Using acrylic paints, paint snowflake onto ornament. When completed, spray with a clear acrylic spray such as Krystal Klear™. Cut a piece of blue fabric ¹/₂" bigger than frame all around. Cut out a small bit of the center, leaving ¹/₂" to fold to the back of the frame. Sew ribbons, buttons and embellishments to the fabric. Cover paper mache frame with blue fabric; glue fabric tightly to back of frame. Add ornament to front of frame by sewing to the fabric.

Gift Bags, Cards and other projects: Print the files **Ornaments_1-3** and trace and paint images or print onto inkjet papers for paper crafts. Embellish with aqua and red perle cotton threads, scrapbooking snowflakes made from beads and lots of ribbons. Enjoy being creative and trying new techniques and embellishments. Gift Bag: Mount painted ornament onto fabric and make lots of French Knots all around for texture. Sew on ribbons and add Scrabble letters to spell "joy."

Listing of all the files on your JennaDisc

4thBigStars.pdf
4thSails.pdf
4thScatter.pdf
4thSmallStars.pdf
Asian1.pdf
Asian2.pdf
Asian3.pdf
Asian4.pdf
Balmshell.pdf
BBQ_1.pdf
BBQ_2.pdf
BBQ_3.pdf
BBQ_4.pdf
Beach_Babes11x17.pdf
Beach_Big_Blue.pdf
Beach_Big_Pink.pdf
Beach_Blue.pdf
Beach_Pink.pdf
Beach_Suntan.pdf
Blue_Stripe.pdf
Citrina1.pdf
Citrina2.pdf
Citrina3.pdf
Citrina7x7.pdf
Citrina11x17.pdf
FallBorder_1.pdf
FallBorder_2.pdf
Halloween_1.pdf
Halloween_2.pdf
Halloween_3.pdf
Heart_Pattern1.pdf
Heart_Pattern2.pdf
Holiday_1.pdf
Holiday_2.pdf
Jam_1.pdf
Jars_1.pdf

Kimono1.pdf
Kimono2.pdf
Kitchen_Witch1.pdf
Kitchen_Witch2.pdf
Kitchen_Witch3.pdf
Meditate.pdf
Navigate.pdf
Orange_Stripe.pdf
Ornaments_1.pdf
Ornaments_2.pdf
Ornaments_3.pdf
Radiate.pdf
SANTA_FACES.pdf
SANTA_Reverse.pdf
SANTA1.pdf
SANTA2.pdf
SANTA3.pdf
SANTA4.pdf
SANTA5.pdf
Splendid_Cookies.pdf
Spring_Flower.pdf
Stocking_Cuff.pdf
Stocking_Pattern1.pdf
Stocking_Pattern2.pdf
Strawberry_Leaves.pdf
Strawberry_Pattern.pdf
talk_1.pdf
talk2.pdf
Trimmings_1.pdf
Trimmings_2.pdf
Trimmings_3.pdf
Trimmings_4.pdf
VINTAGEcollage.pdf
VINTAGEheart.pdf
VINTAGEroses.pdf
VINTAGEtext.pdf

NOTES